Author
Wendy Conklin

Standards
To learn important shifts in today's standards, see the Parent Handbook on pages 119–125. For information on how this resource meets national and other state standards, scan the QR code or visit our website at http://www.shelleducation.com and following the on-screen directions.

Publishing Credits

Corinne Burton, M.A.Ed., *President*; Emily R. Smith, M.A.Ed., *Content Director*; Jennifer Wilson, *Senior Editor*; Robin Erickson, *Multimedia Designer*; Valerie Morales, *Assistant Editor;* Stephanie Bernard, *Assistant Editor*; Amber Goff, *Editorial Assistant*; Mindy Duits, *Cover Concept*

Image Credits

pp. 5–6, p. 12, p. 74, p. 95: iStock; p.45: Daryll Collins; All other images Shutterstock

Standards

Shell Education
5301 Oceanus Drive
Huntington Beach, CA 92649-1030
http://www.shelleducation.com

ISBN 978-1-4258-1553-0

Table of Contents

Welcome to Summer Blast!

Dear Family,

Welcome to *Summer Blast: Getting Ready for Third Grade.* Third grade will be an exciting and challenging year for your child. There will be plenty of new learning opportunities, including more complex books to read and more work with fractions and decimals! Interesting new topics in science and social studies will help keep your child engaged in the lessons at school.

Summer Blast was designed to help solidify the concepts your child learned in second grade and to help your child prepare for the year ahead. The activities are based on today's standards and provide practice with essential skills for the upcoming grade level. Keeping reading, writing, and mathematics skills sharp while your child is on break from school will help his or her third-grade year get off to a great start. This book will help you BLAST through summer learning loss!

Keep these tips in mind as you work with your child this summer:

- Set aside a specific time each day to work on the activities.
- Have your child complete one or two pages each time he or she works, rather than an entire week's worth of activity pages at one time.
- Keep all practice sessions with your child positive and constructive. If the mood becomes tense or you and your child get frustrated, set the book aside and find another time to practice.
- Help your child with instructions, if necessary. If your child is having difficulty understanding what to do, work through some of the problems together.
- Encourage your child to do his or her best work and compliment the effort that goes into learning.

Enjoy spending time with your child during his or her vacation from school, and be sure to help him or her prepare for the next school year. Third grade will be here before you know it!

What Does Your Rising Third Grader Need to Know?

1. Use root words, prefixes, and suffixes to identify new words.
2. Understand figurative language such as similes and metaphors.
3. Use resources such as the Internet and nonfiction books to conduct research.
4. Multiply and divide numbers within 100.
5. Understand fractions.
6. Calculate area and perimeter of two-dimensional shapes.
7. Know how the water cycle works.
8. Understand that Earth and other planets orbit the sun, and that the moon orbits Earth.
9. Know about civic life and politics.
10. Understand selective societies in various continents.

Things to Do as a Family

General Skills

- Make sure your child gets plenty of exercise. Children need about 60 minutes of physical activity each day. The summer months are the perfect time to go swimming, ride bicycles, or play outdoor team sports.
- It's also important for children this age to get plenty of sleep. Children this age need between 9–11 hours of sleep each night. Even in the summer, establish a nightly bedtime routine that involves relaxing activities such as a warm shower or bath or reading a story.

Reading Skills

- Set aside a reading time for the entire family at least once every other day. Help your child choose a book at a comfortable reading level. Take turns reading aloud one page at a time. Be sure to help him or her sound out and define any unfamiliar words.
- After reading, be sure to talk to your child about what he or she read. Encourage your child to share details from the books they read.

Writing Skills

- Set up a writing spot for your child. Have all of his or her writing materials in one special place. Having a designated area to write will help your child see writing as an important activity.
- Encourage your child to keep a daily journal or diary. Have him or her spend 10 minutes a day writing about activities he or she did. The writing should also include his or her thoughts, feelings, likes and dislikes, and so on.

Mathematics Skills

- Have your child help you cook or bake. The kitchen is a great place to learn and practice fractions, multiplication, division, etc. Ask your child questions as you go along. For example: *If we only need to make half of the recipe, how many cups of flour will we need?*
- Include your child in grocery shopping. This is a great place to practice multiplication and division. Use the items in the store to help your child practice these skills. For example: *There are a dozen eggs in one carton. If I buy 3 cartons, how many eggs will I have?*

Summer Reading Log

Directions: Keep track of your summer reading here!

Date	Title	Number of Pages

Top 5 Family Field Trips

A Trip to a Zoo

Bring a blank world map on a clipboard with you. As you visit each animal, have your child read the information placard and determine the original location of the animal or species. Then, have your child write the name of the animal on its location on the map. At the end of your trip, determine which location is home to the greatest number of animals at the zoo.

A Trip to a National Park

The National Park Service has a great program called Junior Rangers. Be sure you check in with the rangers at the visitors center to see what tasks your child can complete to earn a Junior Ranger patch and/or certificate. Before you travel to the park, your child can also go to the WebRangers site (http://www.nps.gov/webrangers/) and check out your vacation spot, play games, and earn virtual rewards!

A Trip to a Museum

Before your trip, create a Bingo card of items you will find at the museum (for example, a mummy, a dinosaur bone, or an item made of clay). Make sure to leave space in each box for your child to write. As you navigate through the museum, have your child write one interesting fact about an item in its space on the card. When he or she gets four items in a row, celebrate the victory! At the end of the day, ask your child which item was the most interesting to him or her.

A Trip to a Farmers Market

Make a game out of a trip to your local farmers market by providing your child with a list of things to find, like a scavenger hunt. You could have him or her look for a vegetable that grows underground, a red fruit bigger than a fist, and so on. This is a great way for kids to discover different fruits, vegetables, and homemade items, as well as a chance to learn about farming and small businesses.

A Trip to a Library

Work with your child to find nonfiction books about an important person. First, ask your child who he or she would like to learn more about. Your child can then use the digital catalog to search for books on that person that match his or her reading level. He or she can choose one or two nonfiction books about the person, check them out, and enjoy learning about someone's life!

Top 5 Family Science Labs

Science Fun for Everyone!—How to Make a Volcano

http://www.sciencefun.org/kidszone/experiments/how-to-make-a-volcano/

Learn about chemical reactions with this simple volcano experiment.

Science Fun—Dancing Raisins

http://scifun.chem.wisc.edu/homeexpts/dancingraisins.htm

Learn about carbonated beverages and carbon dioxide while having fun!

Science Fun—Floating Soap Bubbles

http://scifun.chem.wisc.edu/HomeExpts/SOAPBUBL.html

Learn about these beautiful and fragile spheres.

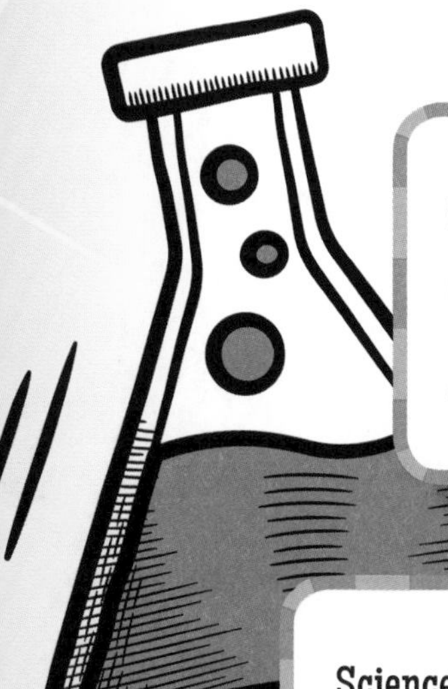

Science Bob—Make a Levitating Orb!

https://sciencebob.com/make-a-levitating-orb/

Learn about static electricity in this fun and easy experiment.

Science Bob—How to Make Slime

http://sciencebob.com/make-some-starch-slime-today/

Learn about solids and liquids as you make your own substance.

Top 5 Family-Friendly Apps and Websites

Apps

Bonza National Geographic by Minimega Pty Ltd

This app includes fun word games and puzzles using facts and images from National Geographic.

Chicktionary by Soap

This fun word game challenges players to unscramble letters to find different words.

Geoboard by The Math Learning Center

The colored "bands" in this unique and fun app teach kids to form line segments, polygons, and learn about angles, perimeter, congruence, fractions, and more!

Websites

Kids Know It Network

http://www.kidsknowit.com

This site features games, activities, worksheets, and information about a number of subjects including history, geography, and spelling.

Funbrain

http://www.funbrain.com/kidscenter.html

Fun, arcade-style games covering a variety of concepts at all grade levels make this a great website for busy families.

Top 5 Games to Play in the Car

I'm Going on a Picnic Memory Game

Start off by saying, "I'm going on a picnic, and I'm bringing . . ." and follow it with an item that starts with the letter *A*, such as *apples*. The next player repeats what the first person says and adds on a *B* item. For example, "I'm going on a picnic, and I'm bringing *apples* and *bananas*." Continue until you complete the entire alphabet. The first person to forget one of the previous items is out. Feel free to adjust the leniency with younger players.

Fortunately/Unfortunately

Begin the game by saying the first a sentence for a story. Then, take turns adding to the story by alternating between the uses of *fortunately* and *unfortunately*. For example, you might start the story by saying, "Amanda went to the zoo one sunny afternoon." The next person would continue the story with, "Unfortunately, the zoo had been taken over by a group of wild monkeys." The next person would add, "Fortunately, Amanda had just graduated from a monkey-training class." Continue alternating between unfortunate and fortunate events.

License Plate Multiplication

Call out the numbers on a license plate and see who can multiply them the fastest! Select two numbers from a license plate and multiply them. You can increase the difficulty by combining the numbers into two-digit numbers. For example, if the license plate number reads 1ABC234, players could multiply 12×3, 13×2, 12×4, or even 12×34. The person who is the first to answer correctly gets a point. The first person to reach 10 points wins! The total can be varied depending on the length of the car ride.

Who Am I?

Think of an important person in history. Give your child a clue about the person's identity by revealing a characteristic, important date, or an event. For example, you could say, "I was president of the United States." Then, answer yes/no questions to give clues about the person's identity. Your child might ask, "Were you the first president of the United States?" Keep answering yes/no questions until the person's identity is guessed correctly.

Yes/No Critical-Thinking Questions

Many verbal games can be played with yes/no questions. Take any game that is traditionally a guessing game (for example, Guess My Number) and make it a yes/no question game. You say, "I'm thinking of a number from 1 to 200." The children have to ask you yes/no questions with math vocabulary. They might say, "Is the number prime?" If the child asks a question without using math vocabulary, don't answer the question. And definitely don't answer if they just take guesses!

Top 5 Books to Read Aloud

Charlotte's Web by E.B. White

This story of a lovable pig, Wilbur, and his spider friend, Charlotte, has been beloved by children and adults for decades. Your child will love the variety of unique characters, as well. This book opens up opportunities to discuss important lessons like friendship and loss.

Because of Winn-Dixie by Kate DiCamillo

A young girl named Opal has just moved to a new town where she realizes it is hard to make new friends. Through the guidance of a lovable dog named Winn-Dixie, Opal learns lessons such as not judging by appearances and how to befriend new people. The themes of unlikely friendships, life in a small town, and family make this a wonderful story to read with your child.

The BFG by Roald Dahl

This imaginative book tells the story of a young girl who befriends a big friendly giant (BFG). The ideas of right, wrong, good, and bad play big roles in the story. Your child will love the eccentric and exciting adventure as well as the lovable character of the BFG.

Freckle Juice by Judy Blume

Reading the story of Andrew and his desperation to have freckles will have your child laughing aloud at Andrew's crazy antics, while instilling the messages of self-confidence and loving your own individuality.

How to Eat Fried Worms by Thomas Rockwell

Your child will enjoy the gross factor of the story of Billy and his friends betting to eat 15 worms. The interesting plot, the different personalities of each character, and the exciting conflict will keep your child engaged and excited to read. The limited illustrations and traditional chapter book structure of this book make it perfect for readers who are ready for a bit of a challenge.

Week 1

This week, blast through summer learning loss by:

- connecting collective nouns
- responding to an article about a game
- writing about trains
- designing a chair
- writing three-digit numbers
- practicing money math problems
- writing expressions
- making a historical grocery list
- using speed to add card values

Name These Groups

Directions: Draw a line to connect each collective noun with its group.

A **collective noun** is a word that names a group of people, places, or things.

1 block	cards
2 bed	flowers
3 deck	houses
4 clump	dirt
5 team	water
6 swarm	bees
7 wave	pancakes
8 stack	horses

Hop to It!

Directions: Read the text. Then, answer the questions.

Here's how to play a fun game called Sack Race. Make two lines about 20 feet (6 meters) apart. One is the start line. One is the finish line. You can use sticks or pieces of rope to make the lines. Have all players line up at one line. Give each player a burlap bag. Each player must step inside the bag and hold on to the top of it. Have someone shout, "Get ready! Get set! Go!" All players must hop to the finish line. The first one to reach it is the winner.

1. List three things you need to play Sack Race.

____

____

____

2. Why did the author write about a sack race?

Ⓐ to explain how to play the game

Ⓑ to explain what a burlap bag is for

Ⓒ to explain how to win the race

Trains

Directions: Read about trains in the early 1800s. Then, write at least three sentences telling how trains have changed over time.

Trains were first used in the early 1800s. They were not like trains today. The cars were like wagons. Horses pulled the cars along the tracks.

In 1830, a new train was made. This train was powered by steam. After this, many railways were made. Most were short-run tracks. This means the tracks were not very long. They carried people from place to place. They carried mail and freight, too.

Later, long railways were made. Trains could travel across the country. The trains had beds on them. This made long trips easier for passengers.

Textiles Extraordinaire!

Directions: You are a talented textile designer. Show your talent by creating a design for the fabric on the chair.

Read Big Numbers

The number 132 has three parts.

•	•••	••

The number for the hundreds goes here. The number for the tens goes here. The number for the ones goes here.

132

Directions: Write the number that is shown by each set of dots.

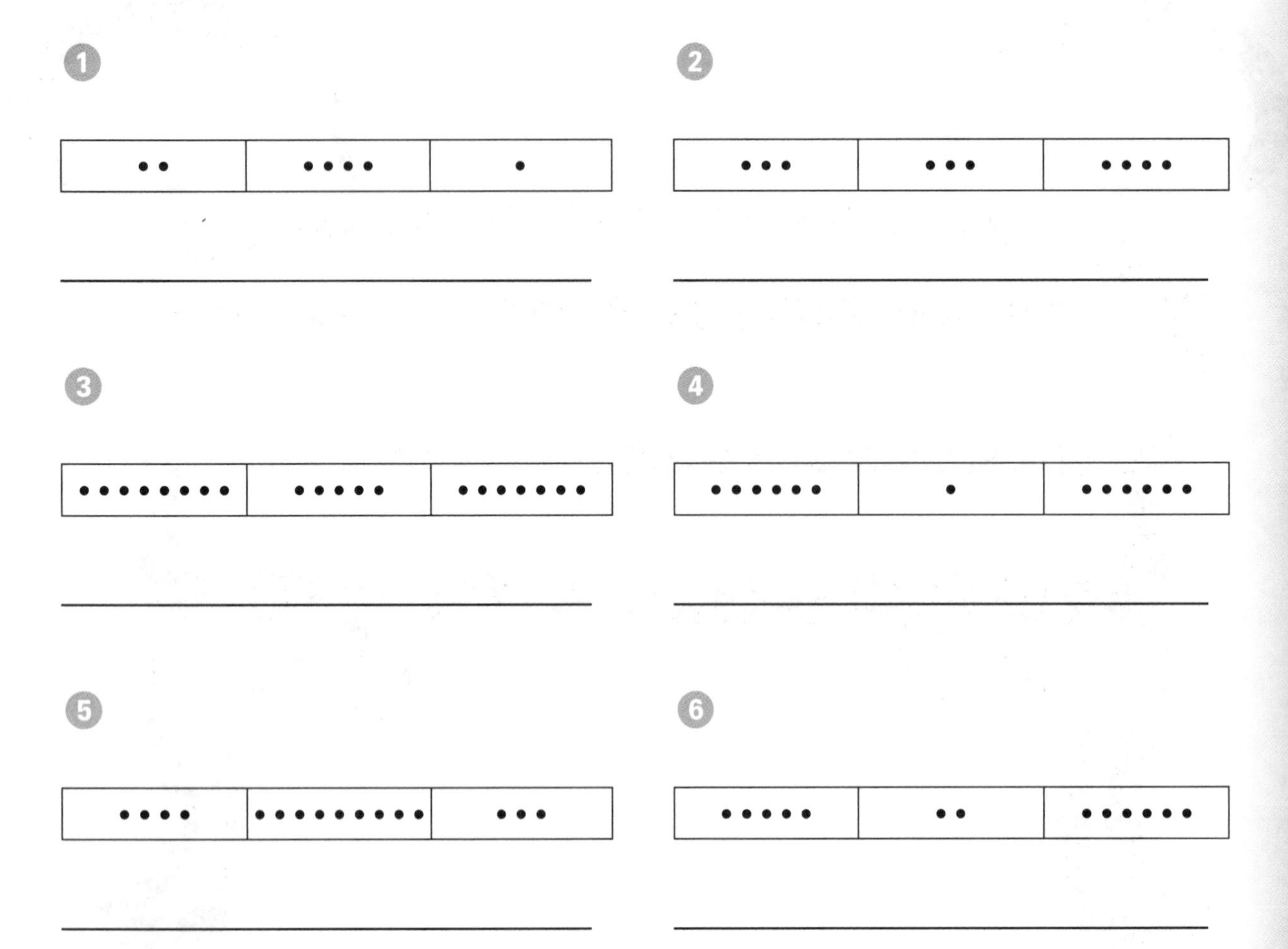

1. | •• | •••• | • |
   |---|---|---|

   ____

2. | ••• | ••• | •••• |
   |---|---|---|

   ____

3. | •••••••• | ••••• | ••••••• |
   |---|---|---|

   ____

4. | •••••• | • | •••••• |
   |---|---|---|

   ____

5. | •••• | ••••••••• | ••• |
   |---|---|---|

   ____

6. | ••••• | •• | •••••• |
   |---|---|---|

   ____

Going to the Grocery Store

Directions: Solve each problem.

1. Sheena has one of each kind of coin. How much are these 4 coins worth?

Value of each coin: _________ _________ _________ _________

Total value: _________

2. A granola bar costs $1. Nia has 5 quarters. Use words, pictures, and numbers to show whether Nina can buy the granola bar.

3. Layla spent 8 nickels riding the bus to the store. Then, she spent 6 dimes buying a drink at the store. Use words, pictures, and numbers to show whether Layla spent more money on the bus or at the store.

Story Problems

Directions: Write an expression to solve each word problem. Draw pictures to help you solve the problems.

1. Crystal has a rock collection of 47 different types of rocks. She gives her friend Sara some rocks so that she could start a collection. Crystal now has 38 rocks in her collection. How many rocks does Sara have?

2. Expression

____

Answer

____

3. Brandon counted 51 vehicles on the drive to visit his grandfather. Of the 51 vehicles, 14 were motorcycles. How many of the 51 vehicles that Brandon counted were not motorcycles?

4. Expression

____

Answer

____

Famous Grocery List

Directions: Imagine you were in charge of making a grocery list of five items for a person from history. Write the name of the person you chose at the top of the list. Then, write the items in the left column. Next to each item, explain why this person would have it on the list.

________________________'s Grocery List

1. ______________ ______________________
____

2. ______________ ______________________
____

3. ______________ ______________________
____

4. ______________ ______________________
____

5. ______________ ______________________
____

Card Addition Game

Number of Players

2

Materials

- deck of cards

Directions

1. Remove the face cards from the deck of cards. Shuffle the remaining cards and place them facedown in a pile.
2. Players take turns flipping over three cards from the top of the pile. Each player should add the three values together.
3. The first player to add the three numbers on the cards correctly gets a point.
4. The first player to reach 10 points is the winner.

Week 2

This week, blast through summer learning loss by:

- finding words that should be capitalized
- responding to questions about a short story
- answering questions about an event
- creating a cartoon about food
- skip-counting with a hundreds chart
- drawing and writing the names of shapes
- guessing and checking to solve problems
- finding unknown numbers
- playing charades

Capital Review

Directions: Underline the words that should be capitalized. **Hint:** There are 42 of them. The first one has been done for you.

1. <u>the</u> first day of school is exciting.
2. freddy wilson's frog, peepers, hopped into mrs. woolsey's purse.
3. the fourth thursday in november is thanksgiving.
4. i like halloween best when it is on a saturday.
5. aunt susan went to yellowstone national park.
6. connie lives on maple street in bismarck, north dakota.
7. brazil, argentina, and peru are in south america.
8. the mediterranean sea and the atlantic ocean touch spain.
9. the letter was signed, "love always, esther."
10. davis medical center opened in january last year.

Lemonade for Sale

Directions: Read the text. Then, answer the questions.

Ann and Lucy wanted to go to the movies. But they did not have money. They tried washing dogs. It was too messy. They tried babysitting. It took too much time. They decided to have a lemonade stand.

The next day was hot and dry. It was a good day for a lemonade stand. The girls mixed the cold drinks. They poured the drinks into a plastic pitcher. They sold the drinks for 50 cents each.

Ten kids and two adults bought the drinks. Ann and Lucy each needed three dollars for the movies. They made enough money. Hooray! They were on their way!

1. Describe a trait that the main characters of this story share?

____

____

____

2. Think of another trait the characters share. How does the author show that trait in the characters?

____

____

____

What Happened?

Directions: Choose one of the events from the list. Pretend you actually did it. Then, answer the questions.

- invented a time machine and had dinner with a famous person from the past
- cleaned up five bags worth of trash in the neighborhood
- collected ten boxes and built a fort

1. What happened just before this event?

____

____

____

____

2. What were you thinking when you decided to do this?

____

____

____

____

3. What happened during the event?

____

____

____

____

Cartoon Foods

Directions: Pretend your favorite food is alive. Draw a cartoon in the frames to show a day in its life.

Practice with Patterns

Directions: Use the hundreds chart to solve the problems.

1	2	3	4	5	6	7	8	9	10
11	12	13	14	15	16	17	18	19	20
21	22	23	24	25	26	27	28	29	30
31	32	33	34	35	36	37	38	39	40
41	42	43	44	45	46	47	48	49	50
51	52	53	54	55	56	57	58	59	60
61	62	63	64	65	66	67	68	69	70
71	72	73	74	75	76	77	78	79	80
81	82	83	84	85	86	87	88	89	90
91	92	93	94	95	96	97	98	99	100

1. Skip-count by fives. Using a blue crayon, shade each box that has a number for counting by fives, starting at 5 and going to 100. What pattern do you see?

____

____

2. Shade the number 83. Start with 83 and count backwards by tens. Using a red crayon, shade in each number for counting backward by tens, from 83 to as close to 0 as you can get. What pattern do you see?

____

____

Sorting Shapes

Directions: Draw and write the names of at least two shapes that fit the description in each box.

1. These shapes each have more than one line of symmetry.	2. These shapes each have all their sides the same lengths.
3. These shapes each have straight sides.	4. These shapes each have an even number of sides.
5. These shapes each have an odd number of sides.	6. These shapes each have an odd number of corners.

Your Best Guess

Directions: Find an item you can measure using the given unit. In each row, make an estimate, make an actual measurement, and write how far away your estimate was from your actual measurement.

Name of Item	Unit	Estimated Measure	Actual Measure	Amount Away from Actual Measure
1	inches			
2	centimeters			
3	feet			
4	meters			
5	millimeters			

What Is the Number?

Directions: Find the unknown numbers. Then, explain how you found the numbers.

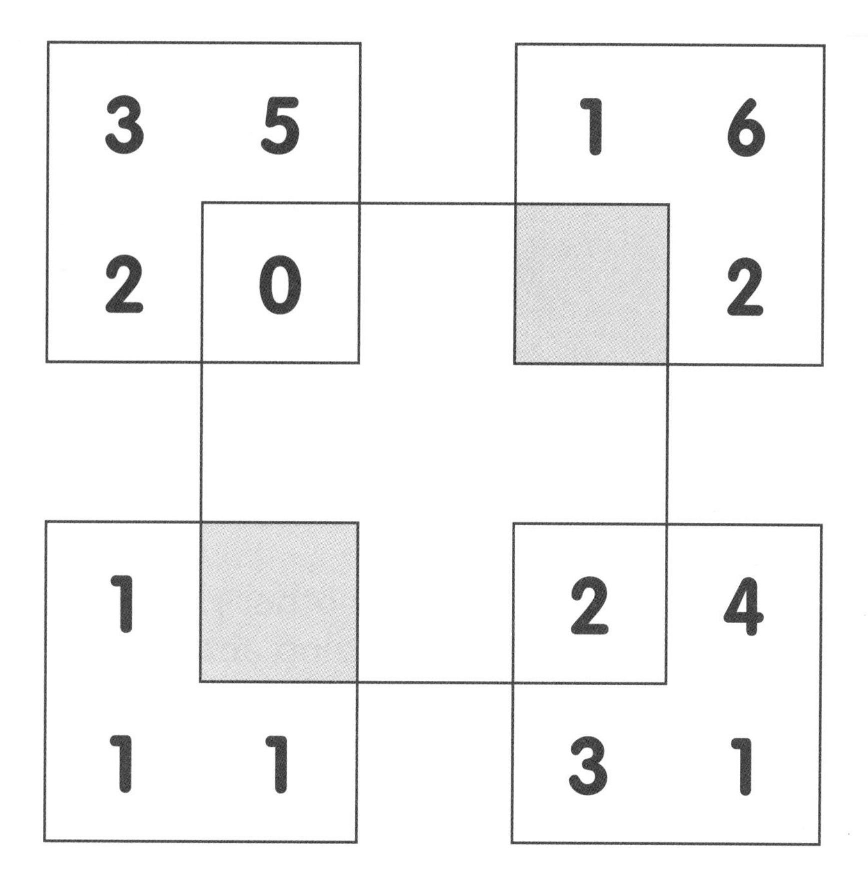

Family Charades

Number of Players

2–6

Materials

- *Action Cards* (page 103)

Directions

1. Cut apart the *Action Cards* on page 103. Shuffle the cards and place them facedown in a pile.
2. Each player takes turns drawing a card and acting out what is written on the card. The player may only use body motions and not words.
3. The other players guess what is being acted out. The first player to correctly guess the action gets the next turn. (**Note:** If players are unable to guess the action in two minutes, the actor may use words to describe the action.)
4. Continue until all cards have been acted out.

Week 3

This week, blast through summer learning loss by:

- writing greetings and closing for letters
- understanding a diagram
- organizing evidence to support statements
- completing an unfinished drawing
- comparing numbers with greater than or less than symbols
- figuring out shapes by their descriptions
- solving word problems
- using context clues to decode mystery words
- playing a category word game

Commas in Letters

Directions: Write greetings and closings for the letters.

____

Can you come to my class play? I would love to see you there. My mom and dad are going, too.

____

____

____

Thank you for my birthday present. I love the books. How did you know I like to read mysteries?

____

____

Can You Hear It?

Directions: Read the diagram. Then, fill in the path below to match the diagram.

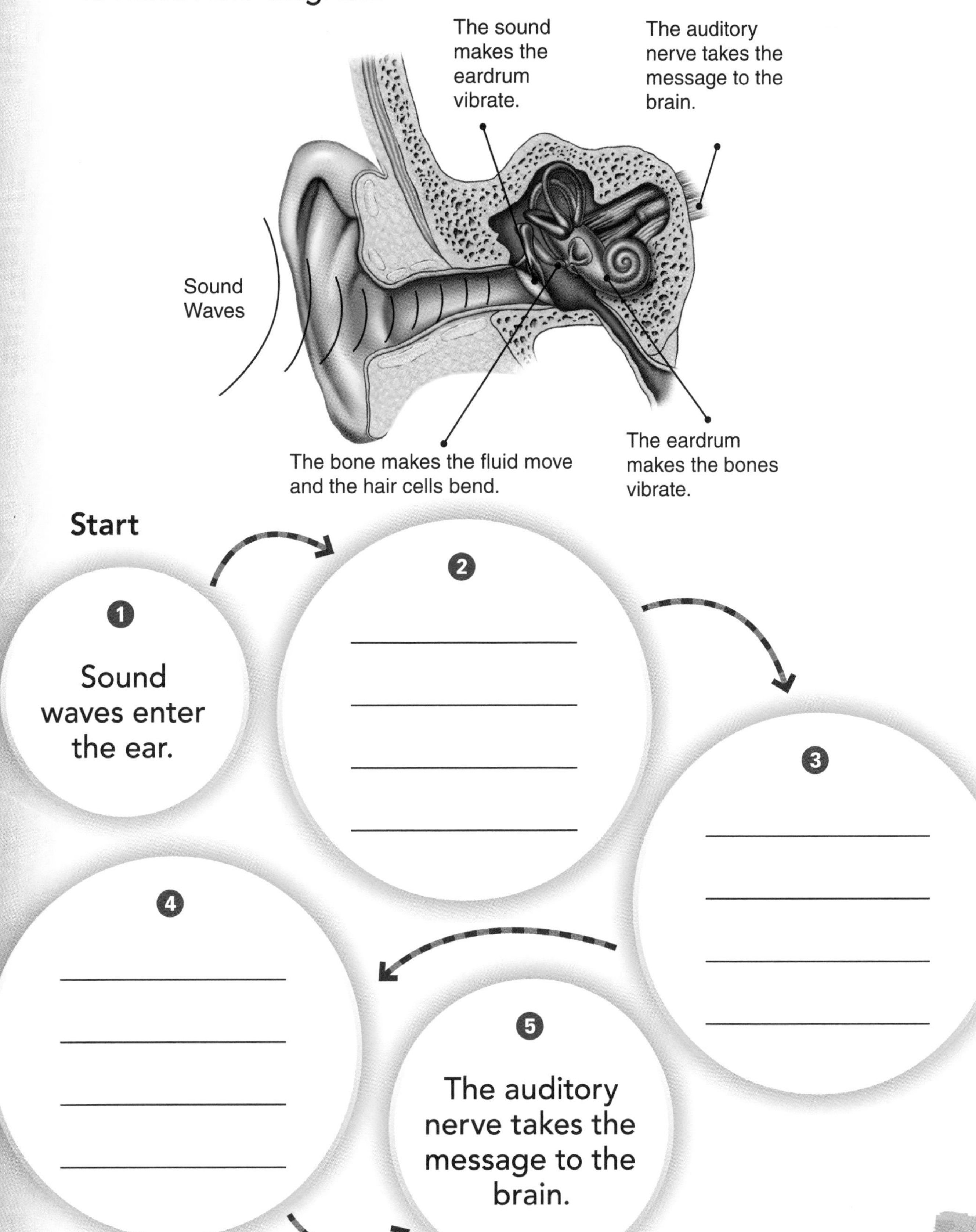
The sound makes the eardrum vibrate.
The auditory nerve takes the message to the brain.
Sound Waves
The bone makes the fluid move and the hair cells bend.
The eardrum makes the bones vibrate.
Start
1
Sound waves enter the ear.
2
3
4
5
The auditory nerve takes the message to the brain.

A Real Hero

Directions: When writing your opinion, it helps to organize your thoughts. Choose a real person or a fictional character that you believe is a hero. Complete this form by writing the evidence to support the statements.

Evidence	
My choice for a real hero is ______________________________ .	
The person takes action.	______________________________ ______________________________
The person is thoughtful.	______________________________ ______________________________
The person makes good choices.	______________________________ ______________________________
The person keeps trying.	______________________________ ______________________________
The person makes sacrifices.	______________________________ ______________________________
The person is loyal.	______________________________ ______________________________

Finish This Drawing

Directions: Use your imagination to finish the drawing.

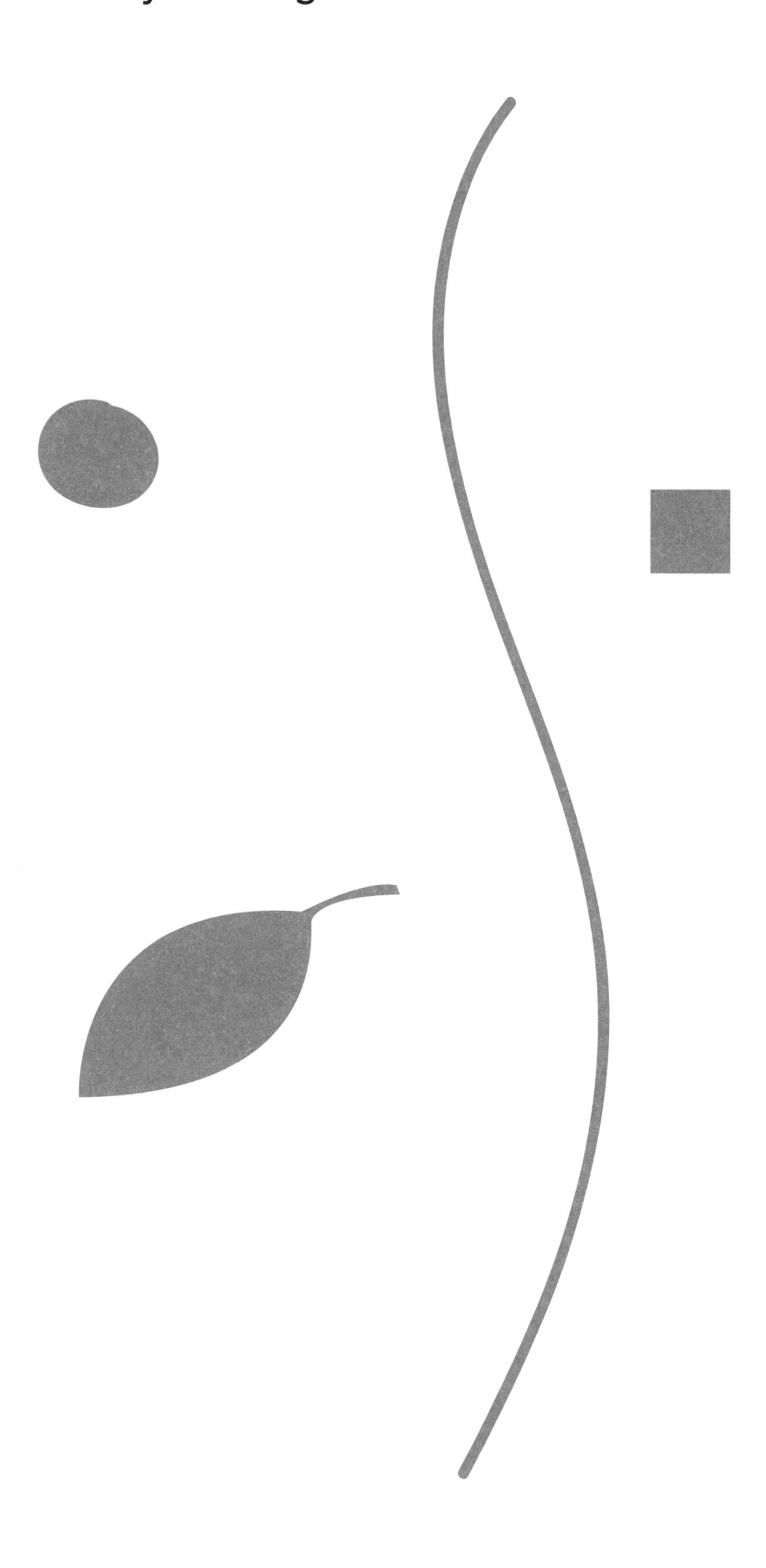

Comparing Numbers

Directions: Write the correct less than or greater than symbol between each pair of numbers.

< is the symbol for less than

> is the symbol for greater than

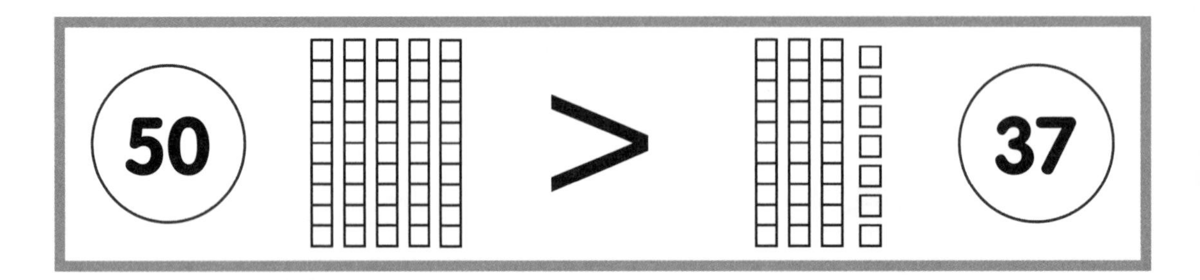

1. 100 ◯ 87
2. 37 ◯ 27
3. 14 ◯ 35
4. 641 ◯ 515
5. 99 ◯ 110
6. 97 ◯ 79
7. 132 ◯ 601
8. 147 ◯ 97
9. 300 ◯ 315
10. 250 ◯ 170

Shape Up

Directions: Solve each problem.

❶ My shape has three sides and three angles. What shape is it?

____

Draw an example.

❷ Draw two different shapes that have four sides and four angles. What do your shapes have in common? What is different about your shapes?

____

____

____

❸ Name the solid figure shown below.

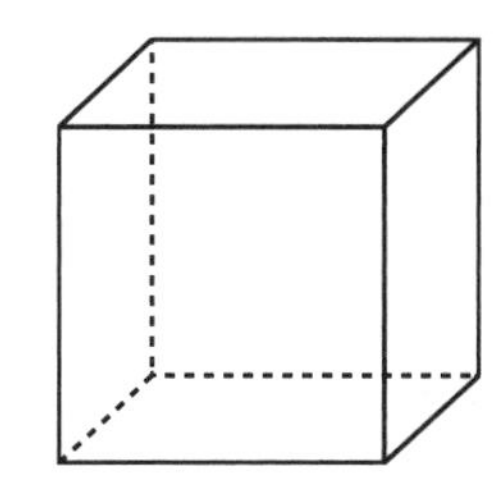

____

The Jungle

Directions: Solve each problem.

1. Tarzan's vine is 25 meters long. Jane's vine is 50 meters long. How long are their vines altogether?

   ____________ + ____________ = ______________________

2. A snake was 39 centimeters long. A month later, the snake is 41 centimeters long. How much did the snake grow in one month?

   ____________ – ____________ = ______________________

3. A tree was 4 feet tall. Many years later, the tree is much taller. It has grown 48 feet. How tall is the tree now?

   ____________ + ____________ = ______________________

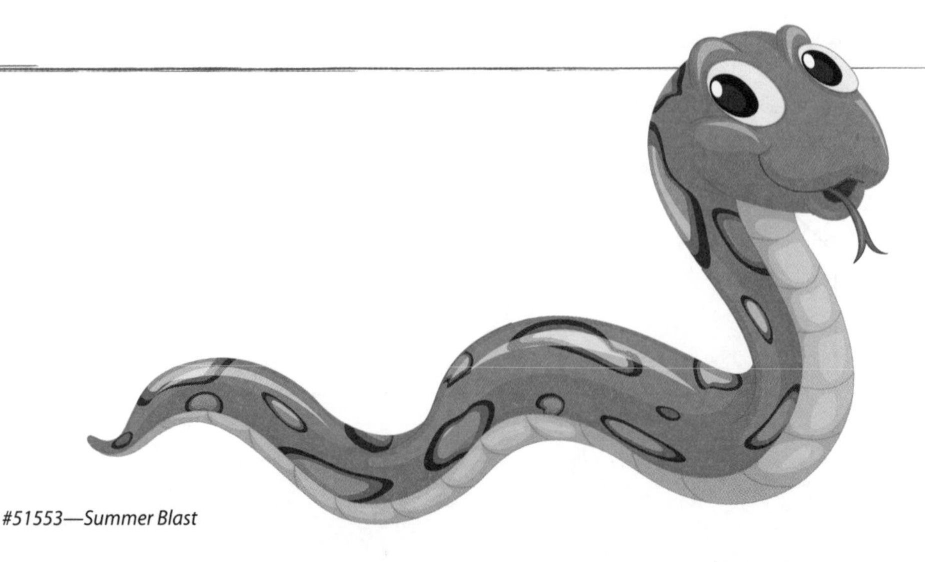

Mystery Talking!

Directions: Can you figure out what the underlined words mean? Use the context clues to determine the meaning of each one. Then, write your answers on the lines.

Hi, my <u>onme</u> is Elizabeth, but every one calls me Liz. I have an adventure to tell you about! I had every intention of getting to school on time, but I lost my <u>qalam</u>. I can't write without my <u>qalam</u>. My <u>athro</u> makes us write all day long. I prefer to use my <u>qalam</u> instead of a <u>bervl</u>. When I make mistakes with my <u>qalam</u>, I use my <u>irabha</u>. A mistake with a <u>bervl</u> is more difficult to correct. Then, I can start over. So, without my <u>qalam</u>, it is useless to go to school!

onme ______________________________

qalam ______________________________

athro ______________________________

bervl ______________________________

irabha ______________________________

How Many Words?

Number of Players

2–6

Materials

- *Letter Cards* (page 105)
- paper
- pens or pencils
- one-minute timer

Directions

1. Cut apart the *Letter Cards* on page 105. Shuffle the cards and place them facedown in a pile.
2. Give a sheet of paper and a pen or pencil to each player.
3. Turn over a letter card and set the timer.
4. Each player has one minute to come up with as many words as they can that begin with the letter on the card.
5. When the timer rings, use the Point System chart below to give each player a score.
6. The first player to reach 20 points wins.

Point System

1–3 letter words = 1

4–5 letter words = 2

6+ letter words = 3

Week 4

This week, blast through summer learning loss by:

- writing prefixes to understand word definitions
- answering questions about a chart
- writing about a vacation
- decorating a birdhouse
- counting stick bundles
- recognizing quadrilaterals
- solving problems using dollar bills
- solving a logic puzzle
- adding numbers using number cubes

Prefix Practice

Directions: Underline the prefixes in the sentences. Then, write the prefixes, root words, and short definitions in the correct columns. Use a dictionary to help you.

Sentence	Prefix	Root	Definition
1 Felix reread the book because it was good.	re	read	read again
2 Leila dialed an incorrect phone number.			
3 Does your sister go to preschool?			
4 Tyler was careful not to misspell any words on the test.			
5 Gina will unpack her suitcase when she gets home.			
6 In health class, we learned not to overeat.			
7 The character in the story was dishonest.			
8 Jose was unhappy when his team lost.			

Using Charts

Directions: Read the chart. Then, fill in the letter next to the correct answer.

Tracking the Weather

Sunday	Monday	Tuesday	Wednesday	Thursday	Friday	Saturday
7	8	9	10	11	12	13
sunny	cloudy	sunny	sunny	rainy	rainy	cloudy

KEY		
sunny	cloudy	rainy

1. The title and chart tell you this is about _____.
   - Ⓐ animals
   - Ⓑ a farm
   - Ⓒ the weather
   - Ⓓ cooking

2. How many cloudy days were tracked?
   - Ⓐ one
   - Ⓑ two
   - Ⓒ three
   - Ⓓ four

3. People who want to know _____ will like this chart.
   - Ⓐ how to cook
   - Ⓑ what time it is
   - Ⓒ what an item costs
   - Ⓓ when it rains

4. Which question does the chart answer?
   - Ⓐ What makes rain?
   - Ⓑ Did it rain on Tuesday?
   - Ⓒ How much does a cookie cost?
   - Ⓓ What is a cloud?

Planning for a Trip

Directions: Think about a time when you were planning for a vacation. Describe all of the things you had to do to get ready for the trip.

The Coolest Birdhouse

Directions: Dress up this drab birdhouse so that it is the coolest birdhouse in the neighborhood. You can add real items to it or simply draw on it.

Ones, Tens, and Hundreds

This bundle shows 100 sticks.

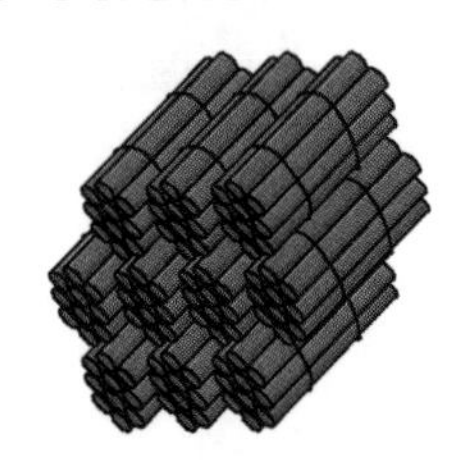

This bundle shows 10 sticks.

This shows 2 sticks.

The number for the hundreds goes here.

The number for the tens goes here.

The number for the ones goes here.

112

Directions: Answer the questions.

1 What number is shown? ______	
2 What number is shown? ______	
3 What number is shown? ______	
4 What number is shown? ______	

Finding Quadrilaterals

Directions: Is the shape a quadrilateral? Circle *Yes* or *No* and name the shape. If the shape is not a quadrilateral, tell why not.

Example: (pentagon)	Yes / (No)	Name: pentagon Why Not? It has 5 sides.
1	(Yes) / No	Name: ________ Why Not? ________
2 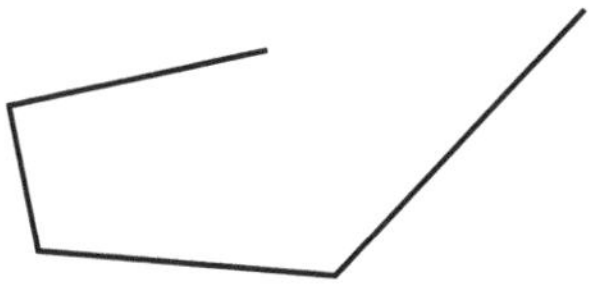	Yes / No	Name: ________ Why Not? ________
3 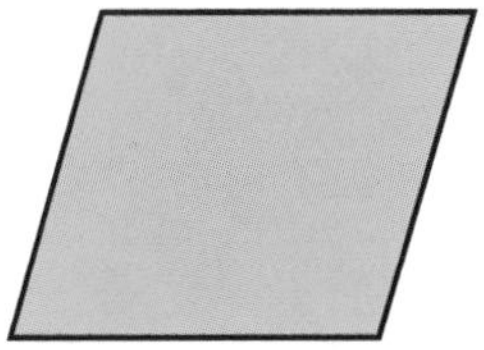	Yes / No	Name: ________ Why Not? ________
4 	Yes / No	Name: ________ Why Not? ________
5	Yes / No	Name: ________ Why Not? ________

Max and His Money

Directions: Max gets $5.00 for allowance each week. Use this information to solve the problems.

1. How much does Max receive in 3 weeks?
   $____________

2. Max wants to buy a model airplane. It costs $20.00. How many weeks of allowance does he need to save $20.00? ____________ weeks

3. Max has $75.00 in his bank account. If he takes out $20.00 for the model airplane, how much will he have left? $____________

4. Max goes to the store. He has $25.00. The model airplane costs $21.50 with tax. He gives the clerk a 20-dollar bill and a 5-dollar bill. How much does he get back? $____________

Who Sat Next to Whom?

Directions: Use the clues to help you solve the logic puzzler to find out.

Clues

John F. Kennedy sat next to the youngest person at the table.

Abraham Lincoln sat next to the first president of the United States.

Martin Luther King Jr. was born in 1929 and was the youngest person at the table.

George Washington was the oldest in the group and sat across from the youngest person.

Number Cubes Addition Game

Number of Players

2–6

Materials

- paper
- pencil
- two number cubes

Directions

1. Each player will need a pencil and a sheet of paper.
2. One player will roll the number cubes. All players should write down the two-digit number. Then, the player rolls the number cubes again.
3. All players will add the two two-digit numbers together and say the answer out loud. The first player to say the correct answer wins that round.
4. Repeat steps 1–3, alternating players who are rolling the number cubes. This is repeated for at least 10 rounds.
5. The player who wins the most rounds wins the game.

Challenge: Add up the totals from the 10 rounds. The first player to find the total wins.

Week 5

This week, blast through summer learning loss by:

- matching present-tense and past-tense verbs
- writing events in logical order
- writing a short narrative
- creating an advertisement for a dream job
- matching equations with pictures
- drawing and writing about a new invention
- estimating measurements
- answering common questions
- designing and building parachutes

Irregular Verbs

Directions: Draw a line from each present-tense verb to its correct irregular past-tense verb.

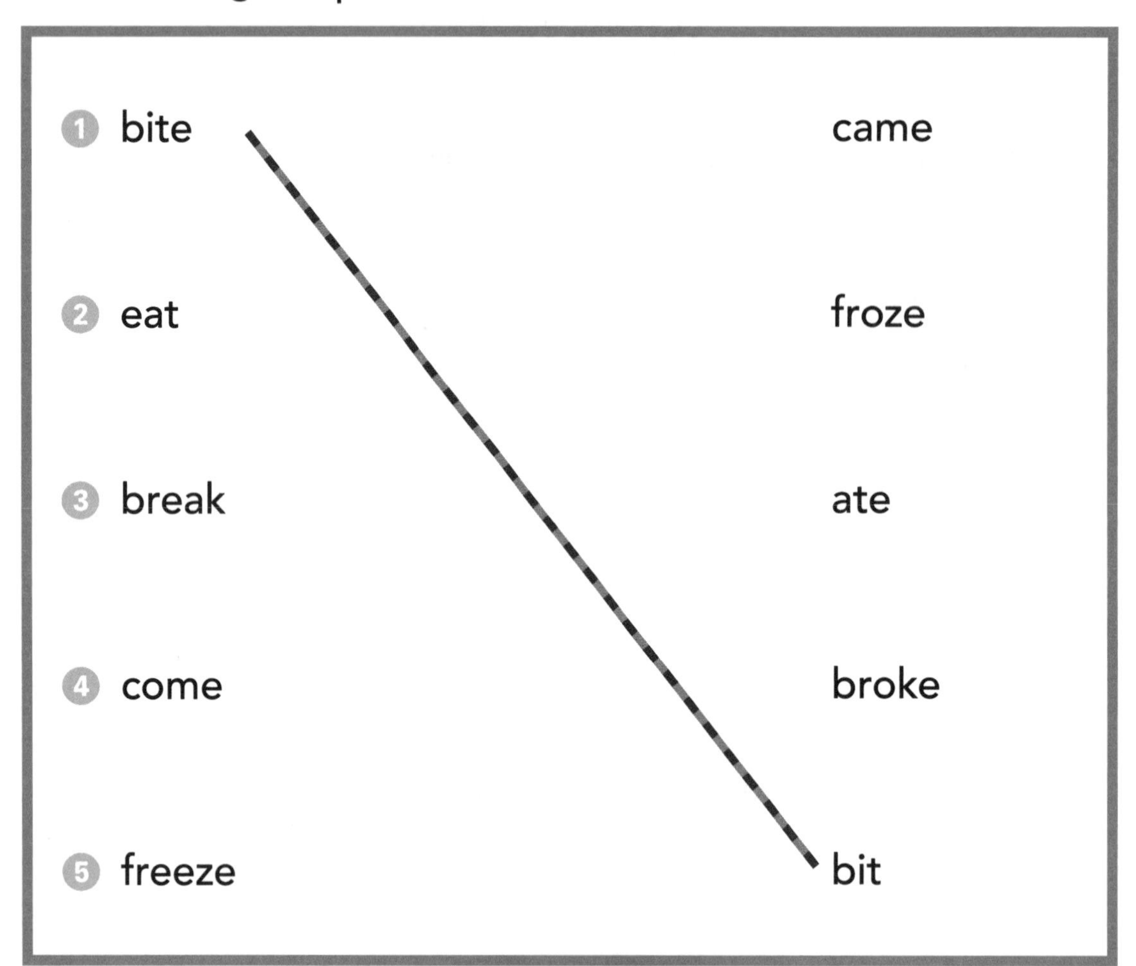

1. bite	came
2. eat	froze
3. break	ate
4. come	broke
5. freeze	bit

The Milkmaid and Her Pail

Directions: Read the text. Then, complete the activity below.

I am Patty the milkmaid. One morning, I was going to market, carrying my milk in a pail on my head. As I went along, I thought about what I would do with the money I would get for the milk.

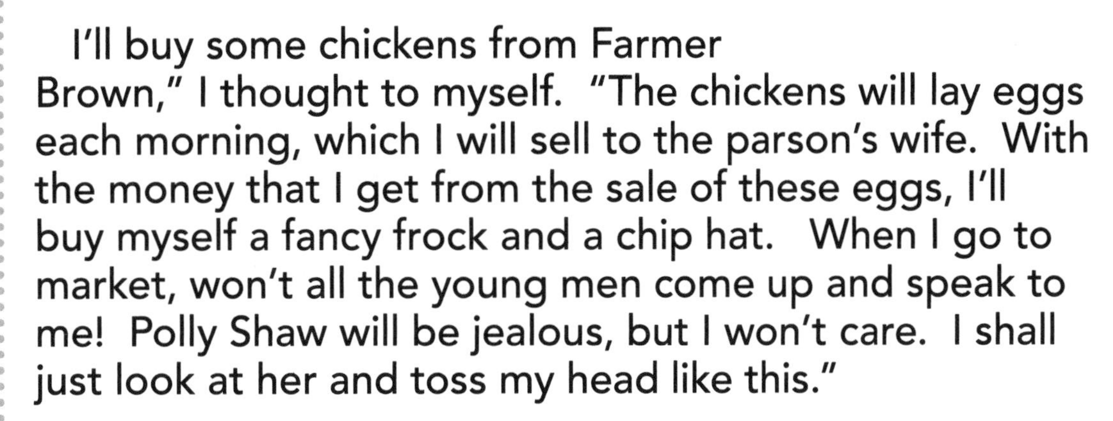

I'll buy some chickens from Farmer Brown," I thought to myself. "The chickens will lay eggs each morning, which I will sell to the parson's wife. With the money that I get from the sale of these eggs, I'll buy myself a fancy frock and a chip hat. When I go to market, won't all the young men come up and speak to me! Polly Shaw will be jealous, but I won't care. I shall just look at her and toss my head like this."

But then disaster happened. As I tossed my head back, the pail fell off. The milk spilled all over the ground.

I had to go home and tell my mother what had happened.

"Ah, my child," my mother said. "Do not count your chickens before they are hatched."

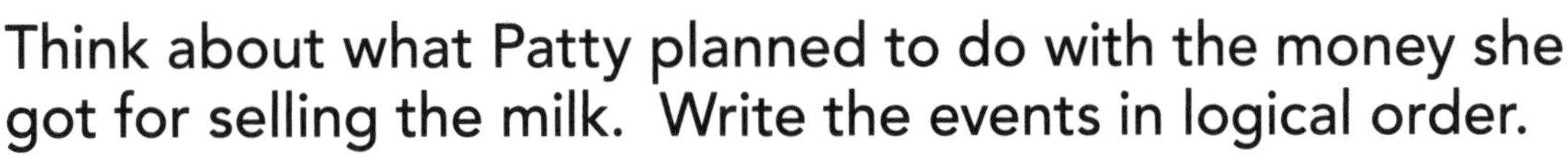

Think about what Patty planned to do with the money she got for selling the milk. Write the events in logical order.

1. ______________________________

2. ______________________________

3. ______________________________

4. ______________________________

Different Places

Directions: Write a narrative about a time when you visited a place that was different from what you expected.

Best Job in the World!

Directions: Think about a dream job you want to have some day. In the space below, use drawings and symbols to advertise this job.

Multiplication Match-Up

Directions: Draw lines to connect the equations to their matching pictures.

Equation	Picture
1.  $5 \times 4 = 20$	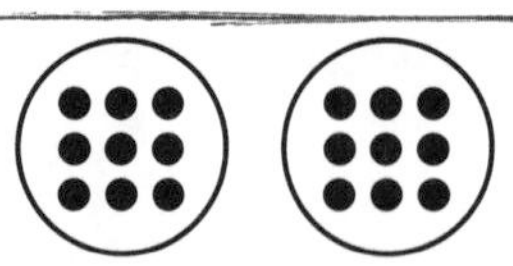
2. $4 \times 5 = 20$	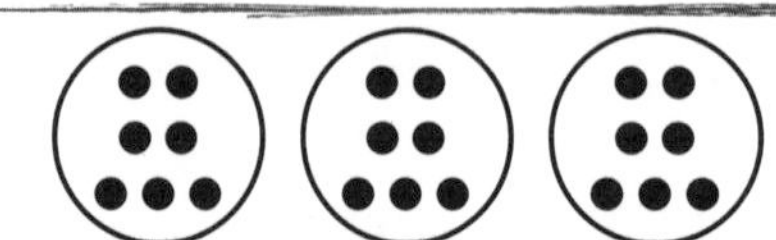
3. $2 \times 9 = 18$	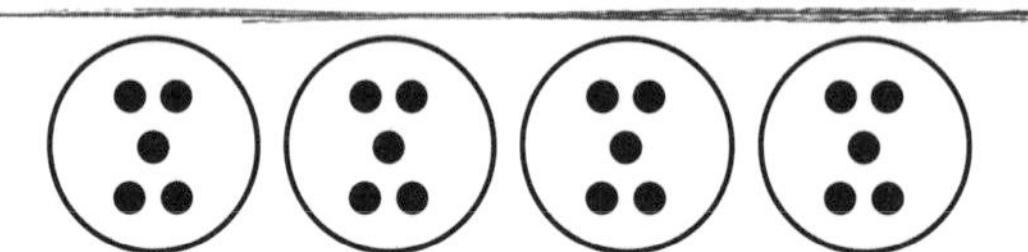
4. $3 \times 7 = 21$	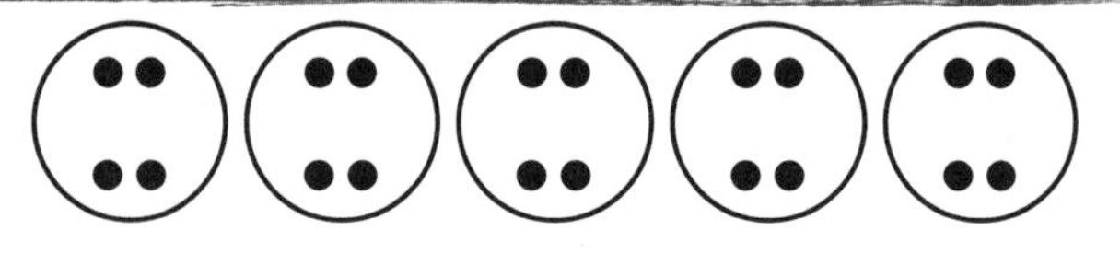

Directions: Solve. Draw a picture to help you.

5. Daria has 6 stuffed animals. Each stuffed animal has 4 legs. How many legs are there in all?

Solution: ______________________________

Three-Dimensional Inventions

Directions: Create a new invention using 3-dimensional shapes. Give your invention a name, and write a sentence to tell what it does. Draw a picture of your invention.

Name of my invention: ______________________________

This is what my invention does: ______________________

____

____

This is a picture of my invention:

Measure Liters

Directions: Choose the best answer to each question.

A **liter** is a metric unit of volume. A shampoo bottle is usually a liter, a soda bottle is usually 2 liters, and a bucket can hold about 5 liters.

1. About how many liters would you need to fill a pet cat's bowl?

   (A) 1
   (B) 5
   (C) 10

2. About how many liters of water would you need to wash your hands?

   (A) 2
   (B) 5
   (C) 10

3. About how many liters of gas are needed to fill a car's gas tank?

   (A) 5
   (B) 10
   (C) 40

4. About how many liters of milk are needed for a baby's cup?

   (A) $\frac{1}{2}$
   (B) 2
   (C) 5

5. About how many liters of juice are needed to fill a large punch bowl?

   (A) 1
   (B) 5
   (C) 10

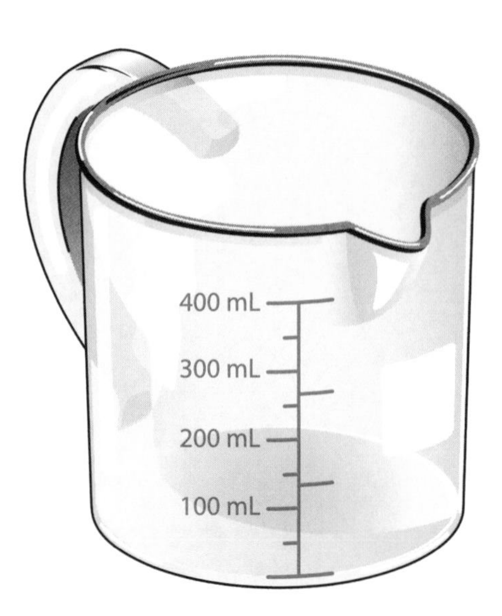

Who Says That?

Directions: Who might ask these common questions?

1. Can I spend the night at Jack's house?

   ____

2. How does it feel when you walk in them?

   ____

3. Do you want paper or plastic?

   ____

4. Do you want salad or soup?

   ____

5. How long have you had that sore throat?

   ____

6. Where is your homework?

   ____

The Best Parachute Design

Number of Players

2–6

Materials

- paper
- plastic cup
- tape
- scissors
- hole puncher
- string
- timer or stopwatch

Directions

1. Give each player paper and a plastic cup to make a parachute.
2. Each player will decide on the size and shape of his or her own parachute. If multiple sheets of paper are needed for the parachute, paper can be taped together. Use scissors as needed.
3. Each player should punch two holes on either side of the parachute. Tie a string from the chute to the plastic cup.
4. Select a distance to drop the parachutes from. For example, have an adult stand on a chair or a ladder.
5. Set the timer once the parachute is dropped. When the parachute reaches the floor, stop the timer. The parachute that takes the longest to drop wins the competition!

Week 6

This week, blast through summer learning loss by:

- defining words
- responding to questions about a letter
- writing an opinion about a game, show, or book
- creating a picture with puppy prints
- using a ruler to compare objects
- dividing rectangles into fractions
- choosing correctly plotted fractions
- solving a word puzzle
- adding cards up to 10

Using the Dictionary

Directions: Circle three words in the text to look up in a dictionary. Then, write each word and its definition on the lines.

As the bread gets hotter, so does a metal wire. The heat causes the wire to bend so far that it strikes a button, releasing a spring and the toasted bread.

1. Word: ______________________

   Definition: ______________________

   ____

2. Word: ______________________

   Definition: ______________________

   ____

3. Word: ______________________

   Definition: ______________________

   ____

Save Our Park!

Directions: Read the text. Then, answer the questions.

November 2, 2016

Dear Editor,

I have lived in Jackson my entire life. I go to Lake School. I am in second grade. I am writing this letter because I do not agree with your article. You wrote about the new shopping mall that will be built on First Street. I think it is exciting to have new things to do here. I just wish our city did not decide to get rid of Hardy Park. Why should we lose a park to get a mall?

Parks are important to everyone who lives here. Kids like to play in them. Adults can relax with their families. They are great places to walk dogs and get exercise. Grown-ups are always telling kids to get more exercise. Are we supposed to get our exercise at the mall now?

Shopping is fun. Exercise is important. I think it is a big mistake to get rid of our park. Some people say that our town has many other parks. This is true. But each park is important. Please, let us keep the park and find another spot for the mall.

Sincerely,
Jamie Smith

1. Jamie's letter . . .
   - (A) impresses her teacher.
   - (B) shares her opinions about parks.
   - (C) stops the mall from being built.
   - (D) gives her exercise.

2. What is Jamie's main point in her letter?
   - (A) People relax at parks.
   - (B) Hardy Park is old.
   - (C) Parks are more important than malls.
   - (D) Shopping is fun.

What Do You Think?

Directions: Choose a book, a television show, or a game. Give your opinion about it. Include reasons why you do or do not like it. Use words such as *because*, *and*, and *also* to connect your ideas. End with a closing sentence.

Puppy Prints Picture

Directions: What can you draw that has puppy prints in it? Use the puppy prints below in a new picture of your choice.

Measuring Practice

Directions: Use a ruler to solve the problems.

1. How many centimeters long is the orange crayon?

   ____

   How many centimeters long is the blue crayon?

   ____

   What is the difference between the lengths of the crayons?

   ____

2. How many inches long is the gray car? ______________

   How many inches long is the green van? ______________

   What is the difference in length between the vehicles?

   ____

Fractions Fun

Directions: Choose four fractions. Divide each rectangle into the appropriate sections, and shade each according to the fraction you chose. Complete the addition problem below each rectangle.

1. 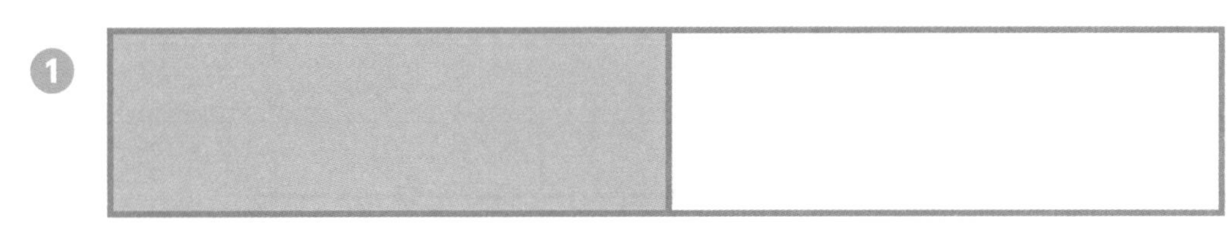

$\frac{1}{2}$ + $\frac{1}{2}$ = 1 whole

2. 

__________ + __________ = 1 whole

3. 

__________ + __________ = 1 whole

4. 

__________ + __________ = 1 whole

Plotting Fractions

Directions: Check that the fraction is correctly plotted on the line. Then, choose True or False.

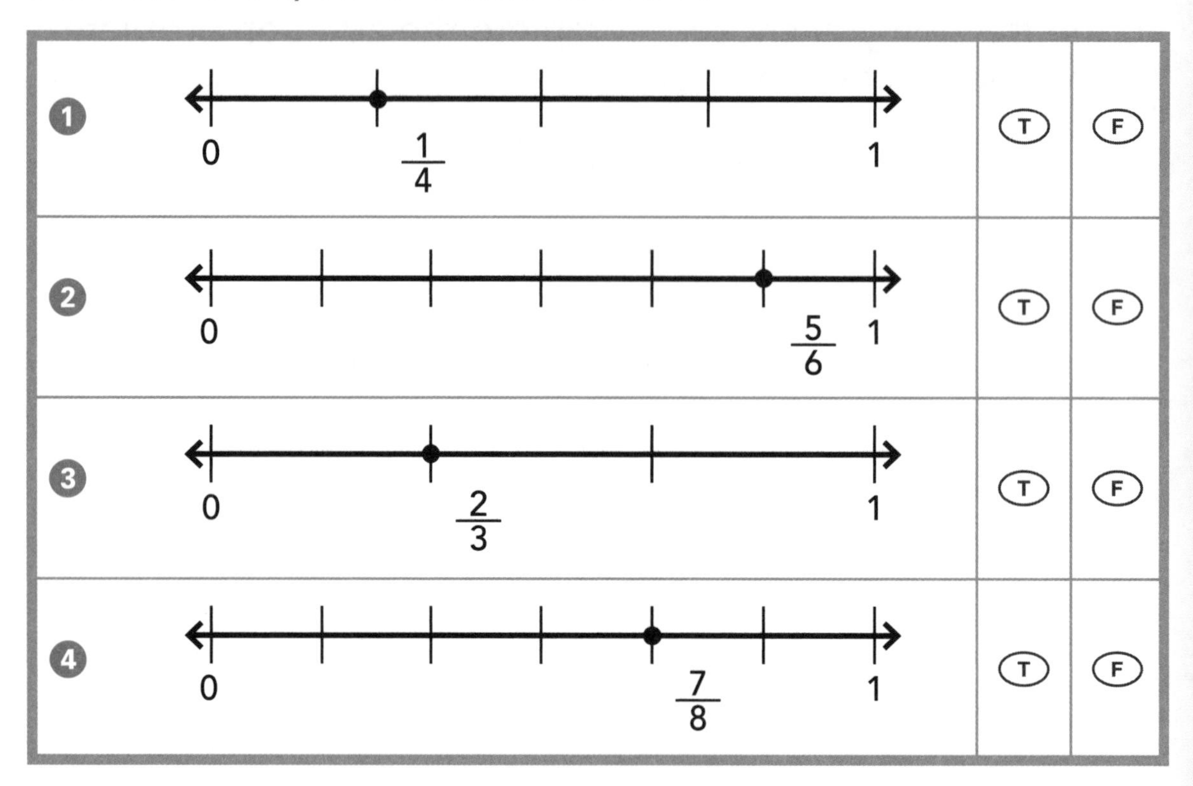

Directions: Plot the fraction on the number line.

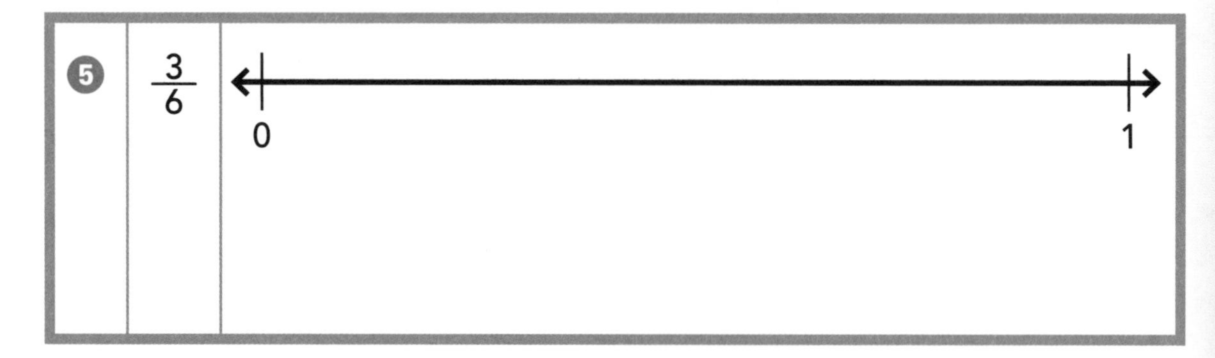

Explain how you plotted the fraction.

____

____

____

What Word Is It?

Directions: Change one letter in each word on the left to make a new word. Use the clues on the right to help you.

Base Word	New Word	Clues
1 lose		You find this on your face.
2 beach		This is a fuzzy fruit.
3 act		This is an insect.
4 jam		This is a container with a lid.
5 hang		This is a loud noise.

The Perfect 10

Number of Players

2–6

Materials

- deck of cards

Directions

1. Remove the face cards and aces from the deck. Shuffle the remaining cards. Distribute three cards to each player.

2. When all players have their cards, players should check if their cards make a perfect 10. For example, a 2 of spades, a 5 of diamonds, and a 3 of clubs equal 10.

3. When a player gets a perfect 10, they get one point and win that round. If no perfect tens can be made with three cards, one more card should be distributed to each player. **Note:** The perfect 10 must be made with three cards. Continue playing until one player makes a perfect 10 with three of his or her cards.

4. The first player to reach 10 points wins. If two or more players tie, have one playoff round.

Week 7

This week, blast through summer learning loss by:

- using suffixes to define words
- answering questions about a story
- writing a poem about an imaginary creature
- commanding a robot
- writing fractions
- solving a fraction word problem
- using a pictograph to answer questions
- completing word sequences
- playing a word sentence game

Hunting for Suffixes!

Directions: Find and circle all the suffixes in the words.

quickly islands slowly
rested breaths caves
badly tried saved

Directions: Think about the root word in each word below. Then, make a prediction about the meaning of the word.

1. powerful: strong, full of power
2. powerless: ____________
3. repower: ____________
4. unpowered: ____________

Challenge: In your own words, write how you can use word parts to help you read and define an unknown word.

____

____

The Horned Owl

Directions: Read the text. Then, answer the questions.

Owls

If you hear "hoo hoo" at night, a great horned owl may be near. Owls do not always live in the woods. Some live right in town. They make their nests in tree holes or stumps. They may even take over another bird's nest!

Owls eat rabbits, squirrels, and other birds. They hunt at night. They swoop down and grab an unlucky animal. They might swallow it whole!

The female great horned owl may lay two or three eggs. The male helps her keep the eggs warm. He also hunts for food.

1. Where does a great horned owl live?

   ____

   ____

2. What do they eat?

   ____

   ____

3. How does the male owl help?

   ____

   ____

My Creature

Directions: Write a poem about an imagined creature. Then, draw your creature.

Robot Orders

Directions: This is your robot. It can do anything you ask it to do. Think about what you would order the robot to do for you. Create drawings and write words around the robot that show what you would have it do.

Picture Fractions

Directions: Write the fraction that shows which portion of each picture is shaded. Then, write the name of the fraction in words.

A **fraction** names part of a whole or a group. The top number is the *numerator*. It tells how many parts of the whole you are describing. The bottom number is the *denominator*. It tells how many equal parts there are in all.

$\frac{1}{2}$ — 1 ← **numerator** (shaded part); 2 ← **denominator** (number of equal parts)

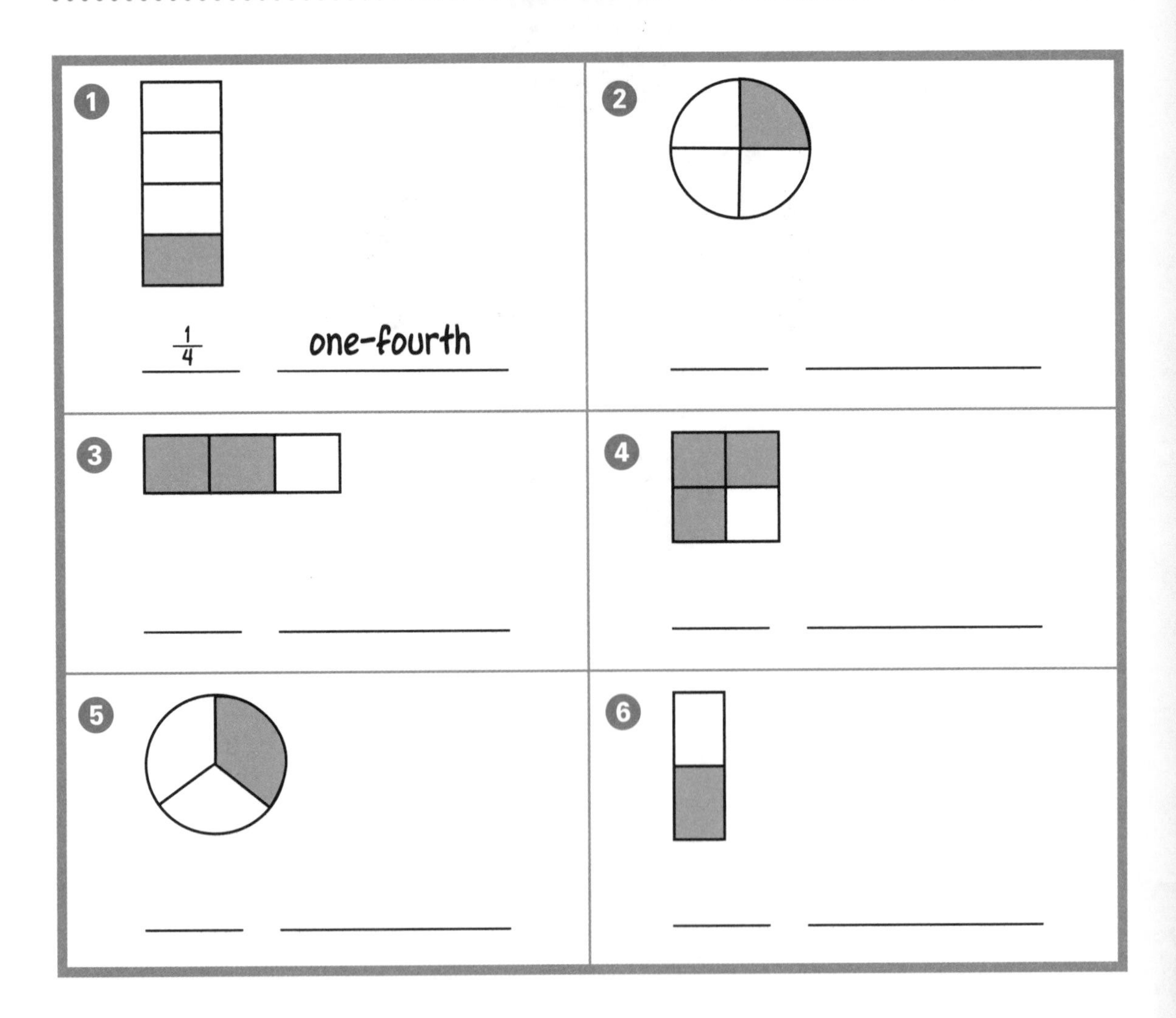

Jog-A-Thon

Jen and Christina are practicing for the school jog-a-thon. They want to train as much as they can. Today, Jen ran $\frac{2}{3}$ of a mile. Christina ran $\frac{3}{5}$ of a mile. Did they run the same distance?

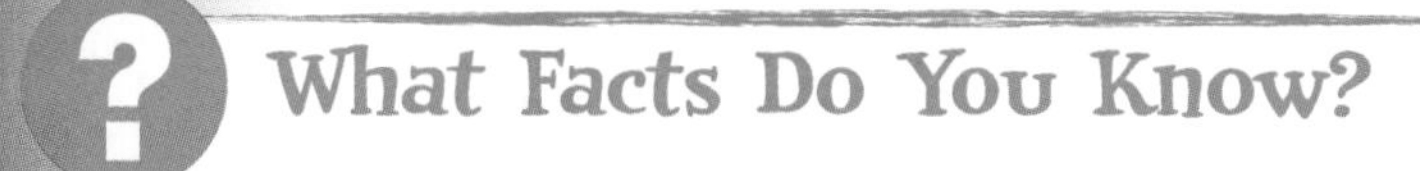
What Facts Do You Know?

How Can You Solve?

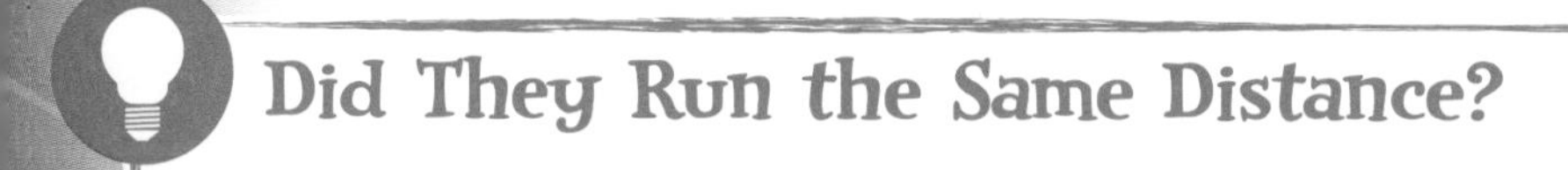
Did They Run the Same Distance?

Explain How You Know

Traffic Survey

Mrs. Johnson's class carried out a traffic survey, recording the color of each car that passed by their window in 10 minutes.

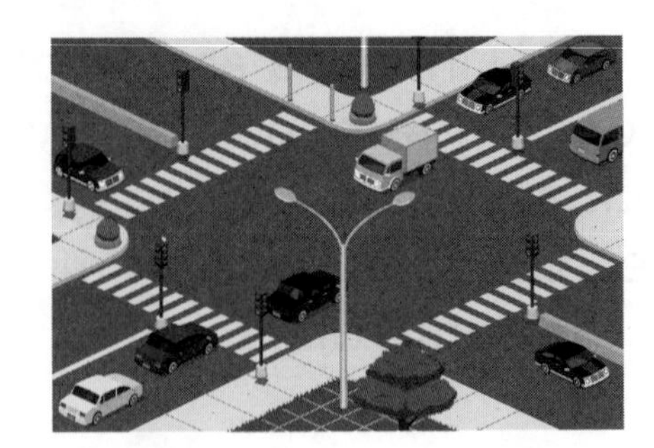

Here are the results:

Car Color	green	blue	red	white	black
Number of Cars	8	6	5	2	9

Directions: Record the information in this pictograph.

[car icon] = 2 cars

Car Color	
black	
white	
red	
blue	
green	

Number of Cars

Directions: Use your pictograph to answer the following questions.

1. Which color car passed by only 2 times? ____________
2. How many more blue than red cars passed by?

   ____
3. Which color car passed by most frequently?

   ____

What Comes Next?

Directions: What word comes next in each sequence? Fill in the blanks with the correct words.

1. morning afternoon evening
2. day week ________________ year
3. Monday Wednesday ________________
4. August July ________________
5. ________________ child teenager adult

Turning Letters into Sentences

Number of Players

2–6

Materials

- *Letter Cards* (pages 107 and 109)
- pencils
- paper
- timer

Directions

1. Each player will need a sheet of paper and a pencil.
2. Cut apart the *Letter Cards* on pages 107 and 109 and place them facedown in a pile.
3. Set the timer for two minutes.
4. One player will turn over four cards to reveal four letters. Players will make a sentence with words that begin with those four letters in any order. For example, the letters are *j*, *a*, *t*, *a*. A player might write the following sentence: Jaguars are tough animals. Another player might write the following: Always jump after turtles. (**Note:** Sentences that do not make sense are okay as long as every letter has a word.)
5. The players who write sentences using the correct letters get one point.
6. Play at least 10 rounds. The player with the most points wins!

Week 8

This week, blast through summer learning loss by:

- separating nouns and verbs
- ordering events in chronological order
- writing about helping the environment
- drawing a home with a slide
- finding perimeter
- reading bar graphs
- plotting fractions on a number line
- rhyming words with names
- using cards to play a multiplication game

Noun or Verb?

Directions: Decide if the words are nouns or verbs. Write each word in the correct column.

Word Bank

add	ant	April	arrive	behave
camera	decide	eagle	exclaim	forgive
holiday	imagine	joy	meal	prepare
prove	ribbon	sky	spider	tree

Nouns	Verbs

The History of Death Valley

Directions: Read the text. Then, number the sentences below in the correct order from 1–5.

American Indians came to Death Valley long ago. But they did not live there all year. Sometimes they camped and hunted in other places. Sometimes they did not go to Death Valley for many years. Today you can find things they left behind. You might find arrowheads and spearheads. You might find bits of pottery, too.

In 1849, other people came to Death Valley. They were looking for gold. They did not plan well for their trip. It was very hot and dry. Many people died in Death Valley. That is how it got its name.

More people came to Death Valley in 1881. They came to mine borax. Borax is a chemical. It is used for cleaning and to make some products. People picked up or dug borax pieces from the ground.

Scotty's Castle is a famous place in Death Valley. It is a ranch house. The house was built in the 1920s by Albert Johnson. It was named for Walter Scott. He was a miner who was Johnson's friend.

Death Valley is famous for its beauty. People wanted it to stay beautiful and natural. It was made a national monument in 1933.

____ Death Valley was made a national monument.

____ People came to Death Valley to mine gold.

____ Scotty's Castle was built.

____ American Indians came to Death Valley.

____ People came to Death Valley to mine borax.

Don't Throw It Away!

Directions: There are many ways you can help the environment. Tell at least three ways that you can reuse, repurpose, or recycle some items in your home.

Slide Winner!

Directions: Congratulations! You have won a slide. Where will you put the slide? Draw a picture of your home and where you will put the slide.

Perimeter

The **perimeter** is the outside measurement of a shape. To find the perimeter, add all four sides together.

5 in.

1 in.

Perimeter = 12 inches

Directions: Find the perimeter for each shape.

1. 4 in.

   3 in.

   Perimeter = __________ inches

2. 10 in.

   2 in.

   Perimeter = __________ inches

3. 10 in.

   1 in.

   Perimeter = __________ inches

4. 6 in.

   3 in.

   Perimeter = __________ inches

Reading Bar Graphs

Dimitri sorted a bag of candy he got from a piñata at his friend's birthday party. He made the following bar graph to show the results.

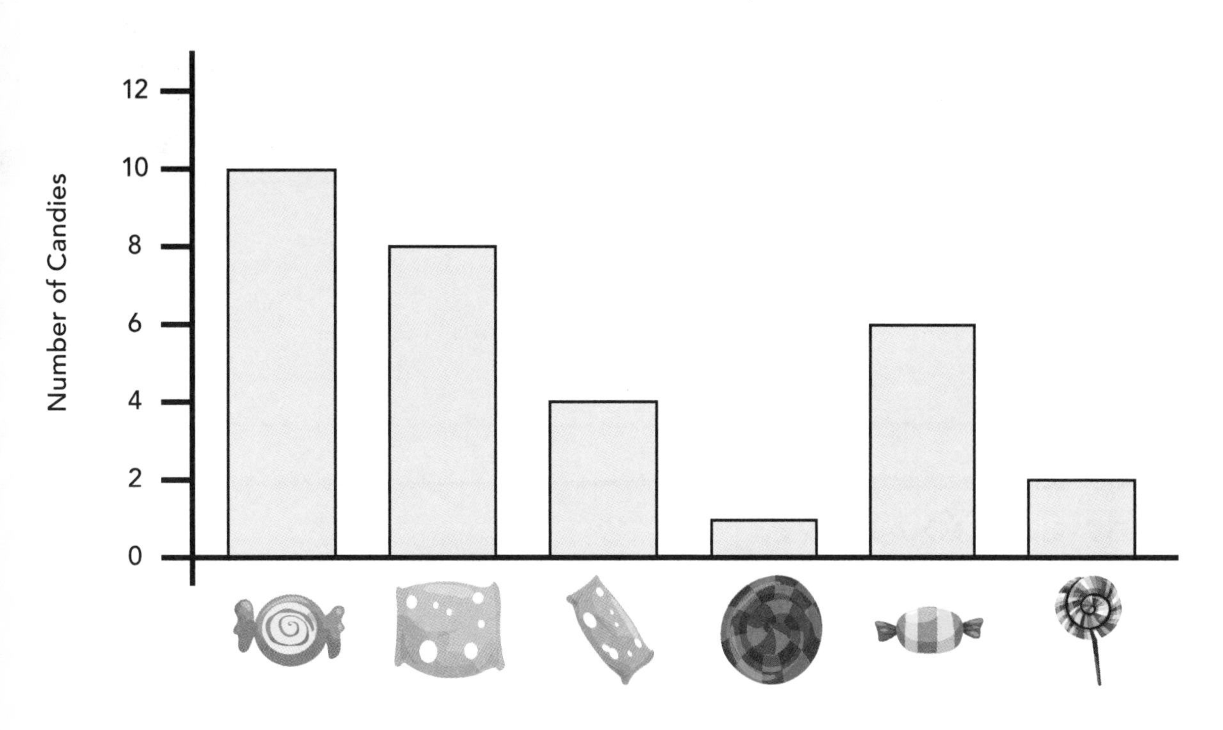

Directions: Complete the table and answer the questions.

Type of Candy						
Frequency						

1. How many ? ____________
2. How many ? ____________
3. How many more than ? ____________
4. Which type of candy occurred least? ____________
5. How many and are there altogether? ____________

Nick and Peyton

Nick and Peyton were talking about where to plot $\frac{4}{8}$ on a number line. Peyton said, "I think $\frac{4}{8}$ can be plotted halfway between 0 and 1." Nick said, "No, $\frac{4}{8}$ should be plotted between $\frac{3}{8}$ and $\frac{5}{8}$."

Figure out who is correct.

What Facts Do You Know?

How Can You Solve?

Who Is Correct?

Explain How You Know

What Rhymes?

Directions: Fill in the blanks with words that rhyme with people's names.

1. Joe, where shall we ________________________?

2. Lori, did you read the ________________________?

3. Marc, can I meet you at the ________________?

4. Jake, do you want a piece of ______________?

5. Joan, can you answer the ________________?

6. Mable, can you wipe down the ______________?

Multiplication Card Game

Number of Players

2–6

Materials

- deck of cards
- paper
- pencils

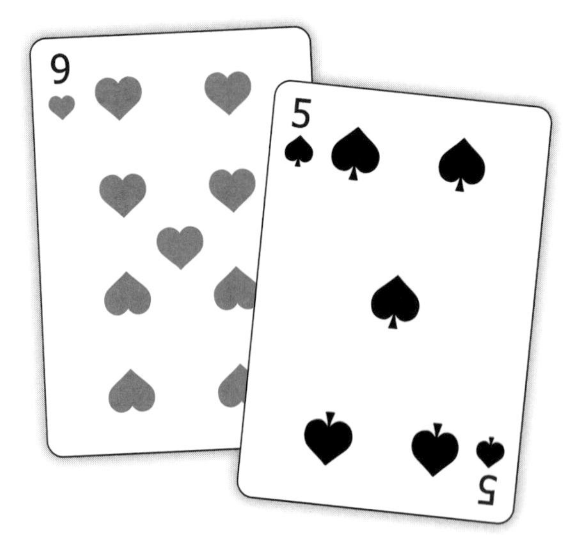

Directions

1. Each player will need a pencil and a sheet of paper.
2. Remove the face cards and the aces. Then, shuffle the remaining cards.
3. Lay the cards facedown in rows so that there are at least 20 cards on the table.
4. Players take turns turning over two cards at a time. The player who flipped the cards multiplies the two numbers together.
5. The other players check to make sure the answer is correct.
6. The next player takes a turn.
7. Continue playing until all the cards have been turned over. The player with the most correct answers wins.

Week 9

This week, blast through summer learning loss by:

- writing contractions
- drawing pictures of what happens in a story
- writing an opinion about chores
- creating an unusual restaurant menu
- estimating and measuring length in centimeters
- practicing telling and writing time
- matching shapes to their descriptions
- matching verbs to images
- playing a number-guessing game

Contraction Action

Directions: Write the correct contraction in each blank.

A **contraction** is a word that combines two words. An apostrophe takes the place of one or more letters.

1. What's your friend's name?
(What is)

2. I think ___________ be sunny tomorrow.
(it will)

3. Our friends said ___________ come with us to the beach.
(they would)

4. Do you know if ___________ food at the beach?
(there is)

5. ___________ going to drive us there?
(Who is)

6. We ___________ taken the bus to the beach.
(could have)

Home Run

Directions: Read the text. Then, complete the activity.

Dear Diary,

Today's baseball game was amazing. The last play of the game was the best. My friend Tara was the batter. Tara nervously stepped up to the plate. She held her favorite bat for good luck. She looked at me and said, "I hope I don't strike out."

Our team needed just one more run. It was hot and late, and the game was tied. The crowd was so quiet. Everyone was watching to see what would happen.

Tara held the bat up high. Leah was the pitcher for the other team. She flashed Tara a grin. She threw her fastest pitch. Tara hit the ball high in the bright afternoon sun. The team cheered, "Home run!"

Directions: Draw pictures in the boxes in the order that they occur.

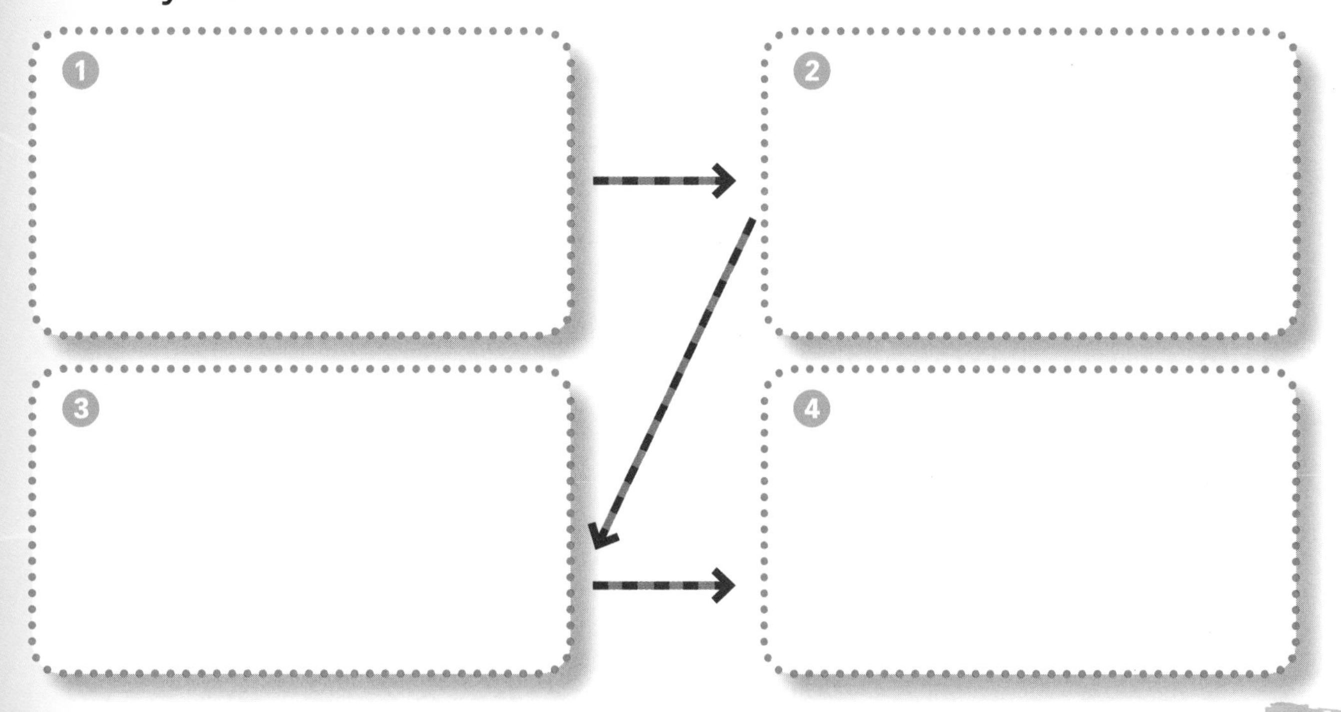

Do We Need Chores?

Directions: Write about whether or not you believe it is important for kids to have chores at home. Be sure to include reasons to support your opinion.

The Most Unusual Restaurant

Directions: You are in charge of creating an unusual menu for a restaurant. What items will you have on it? Create the menu in the space below. Use both words and pictures. Be sure to include prices, too.

Estimating Measurements

Directions: Complete each measurement problem.

1. Estimate the length of the line in centimeters.

My estimate: __________ Actual: __________

2. Estimate the length of the fish in inches.

My estimate: __________ Actual: __________

Digital and Analog

Directions: Complete the chart.

Digital	Analog	Clock Face

	10 minutes to 7	
12:45		
5:55		
	11 minutes after 3	
4:49		
	26 minutes to 7	

Shape Riddles

Directions: Answer the questions. Choose your answer from the shapes below.

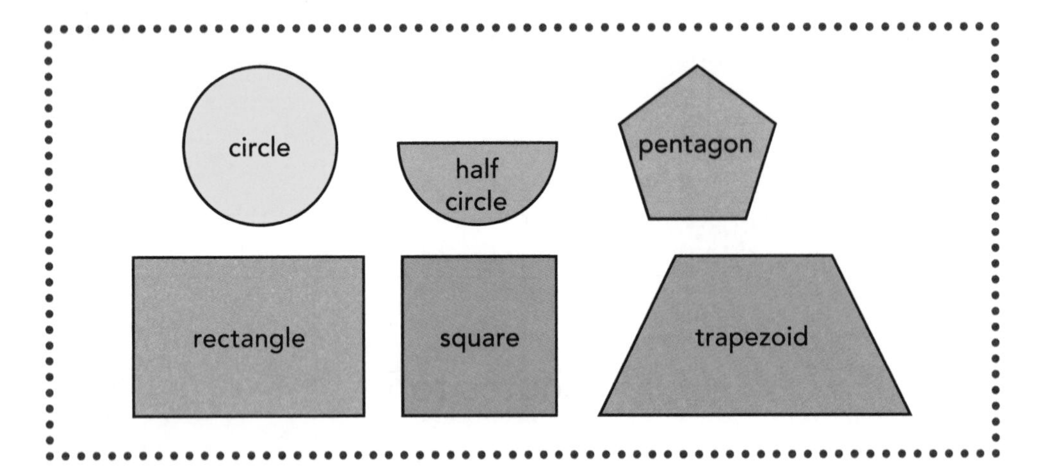

1. I have 4 straight sides. My sides are parallel. My sides are the same length.	I am a ________________
2. I have 4 straight sides. Two are parallel. Two are not parallel.	I am a ________________
3. I am made of 1 line that curves. When you see me, you cannot find where I begin or end.	I am a ________________
4. I have 5 straight sides. My sides are the same length.	I am a ________________
5. I have 1 line that curves and 1 line that is straight.	I am a ________________

Verb Puzzlers

Directions: Write a word from the Word Bank in each box to match the picture.

Word Bank

sizzle	scream	swimming
shower	shine	slip

Guess the Number Game

Number of Players

2

Materials

- paper
- pencils

Directions

1. Player 1 secretly writes a number between 1 and 100.
2. Player 2 writes down a guess of that number and shows it to Player 1.
3. Player 1 says if that number is greater than or less than the secret number.
4. Player 2 makes another guess and Player 1 continues to give clues.
5. The game continues until Player 2 has either guessed the correct number or has guessed 8 times.
6. Then, Player 2 writes down a secret number for Player 1 to guess.

Action Cards

Directions: Use these cards with the *Family Charades* game on page 32.

adding and subtracting numbers	participating in a spelling bee
visiting the school library	teaching a classroom of children
playing at recess	running a race in gym class
reading your favorite book	eating lunch in the school cafeteria
playing an instrument	working on the computer

Family Charades

Family Charades

Family Charades

Family Charades

Family Charades

Family Charades

Family Charades

Family Charades

Family Charades

Family Charades

Letter Cards

Directions: Use these cards with the *How Many Words?* game on page 42.

A	B	C	D
E	F	G	H
I	J	K	L
M	N	O	P
Q	R	S	T
U	V	W	X
Y	Z		

How Many Words? | How Many Words? | How Many Words? | How Many Words?

How Many Words? | How Many Words? | How Many Words? | How Many Words?

How Many Words? | How Many Words? | How Many Words? | How Many Words?

How Many Words? | How Many Words? | How Many Words? | How Many Words?

How Many Words? | How Many Words? | How Many Words? | How Many Words?

How Many Words? | How Many Words? | How Many Words? | How Many Words?

How Many Words? | How Many Words?

Letter Cards

Directions: Cut apart the letters to use in the *Turning Letters into Sentences* game on page 82.

f	p	m	a
g	z	w	x
t	a	l	s
j	n	i	h
k	l	i	m
x	w	v	p
y	z	a	l
h	a	b	f
i	u	c	i

Turning Letters into Sentences	Turning Letters into Sentences	Turning Letters into Sentences	Turning Letters into Sentences
Turning Letters into Sentences	Turning Letters into Sentences	Turning Letters into Sentences	Turning Letters into Sentences
Turning Letters into Sentences	Turning Letters into Sentences	Turning Letters into Sentences	Turning Letters into Sentences
Turning Letters into Sentences	Turning Letters into Sentences	Turning Letters into Sentences	Turning Letters into Sentences
Turning Letters into Sentences	Turning Letters into Sentences	Turning Letters into Sentences	Turning Letters into Sentences
Turning Letters into Sentences	Turning Letters into Sentences	Turning Letters into Sentences	Turning Letters into Sentences
Turning Letters into Sentences	Turning Letters into Sentences	Turning Letters into Sentences	Turning Letters into Sentences
Turning Letters into Sentences	Turning Letters into Sentences	Turning Letters into Sentences	Turning Letters into Sentences
Turning Letters into Sentences	Turning Letters into Sentences	Turning Letters into Sentences	Turning Letters into Sentences

Letter Cards *(cont.)*

Directions: Cut apart the letters to use in the *Turning Letters into Sentences* game on page 82.

w	r	f	n
k	l	r	d
d	a	p	n
e	v	r	q
t	d	e	f
c	i	p	s
q	l	m	n
r	q	o	p

Turning Letters into Sentences	*Turning Letters into Sentences*	*Turning Letters into Sentences*	*Turning Letters into Sentences*
Turning Letters into Sentences	*Turning Letters into Sentences*	*Turning Letters into Sentences*	*Turning Letters into Sentences*
Turning Letters into Sentences	*Turning Letters into Sentences*	*Turning Letters into Sentences*	*Turning Letters into Sentences*
Turning Letters into Sentences	*Turning Letters into Sentences*	*Turning Letters into Sentences*	*Turning Letters into Sentences*
Turning Letters into Sentences	*Turning Letters into Sentences*	*Turning Letters into Sentences*	*Turning Letters into Sentences*
Turning Letters into Sentences	*Turning Letters into Sentences*	*Turning Letters into Sentences*	*Turning Letters into Sentences*
Turning Letters into Sentences	*Turning Letters into Sentences*	*Turning Letters into Sentences*	*Turning Letters into Sentences*
Turning Letters into Sentences	*Turning Letters into Sentences*	*Turning Letters into Sentences*	*Turning Letters into Sentences*
Turning Letters into Sentences	*Turning Letters into Sentences*	*Turning Letters into Sentences*	*Turning Letters into Sentences*

Answer Key

Week 1

Name These Groups (page 14)

1. block—houses
2. bed—flowers
3. deck—cards
4. clump—dirt
5. team—horses
6. swarm—bees
7. wave—water
8. stack—pancakes

Hop to It! (page 15)

1. burlap bags and sticks or pieces of rope
2. A

Trains (page 16)

Check that response includes differences and similarities between trains from the 1800s and today.

Textiles Extraordinaire! (page 17)

Check that the design includes various colors, shapes, etc.

Read Big Numbers (page 18)

1. 241
2. 334
3. 857
4. 616
5. 493
6. 526

Going to the Grocery Store (page 19)

1. Value of each coin: quarter: 25¢, dime: 10¢, nickel: 5¢, penny: 1¢
   Total value: 41¢
2. Yes, because 4 quarters is equal to $1. Nia has 5 quarters, which is greater than $1.
3. 5¢ + 5¢ + 5¢ + 5¢ + 5¢ + 5¢ + 5¢ + 5¢ = 40¢
   10¢ + 10¢ +10¢ +10¢ +10¢ +10¢ = 60¢
   40¢ < 60¢
   Layla spent more money at the store than on the bus.

Story Problems (page 20)

1. 47 – ? = 38
2. Crystal gave Sara 9 rocks.
3. 51 – 14 = ?
4. 37 vehicles were not motorcycles.

Famous Grocery List (page 21)

Check that response includes five items and explanations as to why each item was chosen.

Card Addition Game (page 22)

Check that the card number values have been added correctly.

Week 2

Capital Review (page 24)

1. The
2. Freddy Wilson's; Peepers; Mrs. Woolsey's
3. The; Thursday; November; Thanksgiving
4. I; Halloween; Saturday
5. Aunt Susan; Yellowstone National Park
6. Connie; Maple Street; Bismarck; North Dakota
7. Brazil; Argentina; Peru; South America
8. The; Mediterranean Sea; Atlantic Ocean; Spain
9. The; Love; Esther
10. Davis Medical Center; January

Lemonade for Sale (page 25)

1. Possible answer: The main characters are both hardworking.
2. Possible answer: The author shows the characters trying lots of ways to make money to go to the movies.

What Happened? (page 26)

1. Check that response includes something that would have occurred just before the chosen event.
2. Response should include thoughts on why the decision was made.
3. Check that response includes one of the events listed.

Answer Key *(cont.)*

Cartoon Foods (page 27)

Check that cartoon includes drawings, dialogue, action bubbles, and so on to show the food's life.

Practice with Patterns (page 28)

1.

1	2	3	4	**5**	6	7	8	9	**10**
11	12	13	14	**15**	16	17	18	19	**20**
21	22	23	24	**25**	26	27	28	29	**30**
31	32	33	34	**35**	36	37	38	39	**40**
41	42	43	44	**45**	46	47	48	49	**50**
51	52	53	54	**55**	56	57	58	59	**60**
61	62	63	64	**65**	66	67	68	69	**70**
71	72	73	74	**75**	76	77	78	79	**80**
81	82	83	84	**85**	86	87	88	89	**90**
91	92	93	94	**95**	96	97	98	99	**100**

Possible answer: The pattern I see is the ones place ends in 5, then 0, then 5, then 0.

2.

1	2	**3**	4	5	6	7	8	9	10
11	12	**13**	14	15	16	17	18	19	20
21	22	**23**	24	25	26	27	28	29	30
31	32	**33**	34	35	36	37	38	39	40
41	42	**43**	44	45	46	47	48	49	50
51	52	**53**	54	55	56	57	58	59	60
61	62	**63**	64	65	66	67	68	69	70
71	72	**73**	74	75	76	77	78	79	80
81	82	**83**	84	85	86	87	88	89	90
91	92	93	94	95	96	97	98	99	100

Possible answer: The pattern I see is the ones place stays the same, and the tens place decreases by 1.

Sorting Shapes (page 29)

Possible answer:

1. 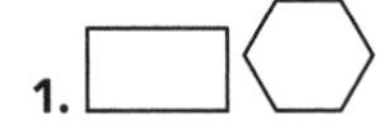

rectangle hexagon

2. 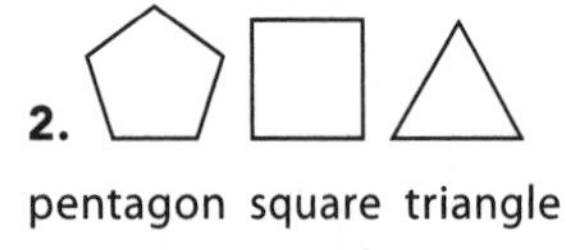

pentagon square triangle

3. 

hexagon triangle

4.

octagon rectangle

5. 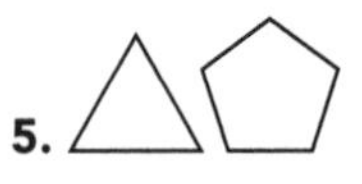

triangle pentagon

6. 

triangle hexagon

Your Best Guess (page 30)

Check that the estimations get closer and closer as the objects are measured.

What Is the Number? (page 31)

The answers are 1 and 7. All of the numbers in each box should add up to ten.

Family Charades (page 32)

Check that actions match the descriptions on the cards.

Week 3

Commas in Letters (page 34)

1. Greeting example: Dear _______
   Closing example: Sincerely
2. Greeting example: Dear _______
   Closing examples: Love; Sincerely

Can You Hear It? (page 35)

1. Sound waves enter the ear.
2. The sound makes the eardrum vibrate.
3. The bone makes the fluid move and the hair cells bend.
4. The eardrum makes the bones vibrate.
5. The auditory nerve takes the message to the brain.

A Real Hero (page 36)

Check that response includes proper evidence for the chosen hero.

Finish This Drawing (page 37)

Check that drawing incorporates the dot, squiggle, square, and leaf.

Answer Key *(cont.)*

Comparing Numbers (page 38)

1. >
2. >
3. <
4. >
5. <
6. >
7. <
8. >
9. <
10. >

Shape Up (page 39)

1. triangle

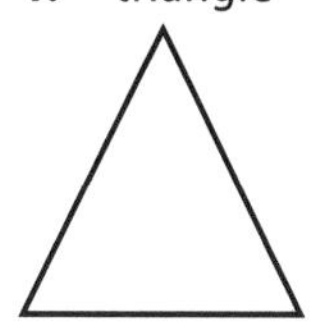

2. Check that answer includes what the two four-sided shapes have in common and how they are different.
3. cube

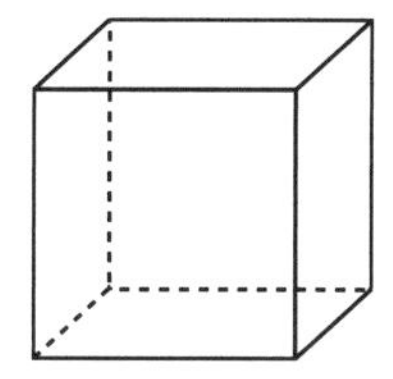

The Jungle (page 40)

1. 25 + 50 = 75 meters
2. 41 – 39 = 2 centimeters
3. 4 + 48 = 52 feet

Mystery Talking! (page 41)

onme: name

qalam: pencil

athro: teacher

bervl: pen

irabha: eraser

How Many Words? (page 42)

Check that the winner has words for each letter chosen and that points are added up correctly.

Week 4

Prefix Practice (page 44)

1. reread; re; read; read again
2. incorrect; in; correct; not correct
3. preschool; pre; school; school children go to before kindergarten
4. misspell; mis; spell; spell incorrectly
5. unpack; un; pack; take things out of a packed bag
6. overeat; over; eat; eat too much
7. dishonest; dis; honest; not honest
8. unhappy; un; happy; not happy

Using Charts (page 45)

1. C
2. B
3. D
4. B

Planning for a Trip (page 46)

Check that response includes details about getting ready for a vacation.

The Coolest Birdhouse (page 47)

Check that the birdhouse is improved with drawings or real objects.

Answer Key *(cont.)*

Ones, Tens, and Hundreds (page 48)

1. 132
2. 115
3. 164
4. 121

Finding Quadrilaterals (page 49)

1. Yes; Name: rectangle
2. No; Why Not? The shape is open, not closed.
3. Yes; Name: rhombus
4. No; Why Not? One of the shape's sides is curved, not straight.
5. Yes; Name: square

Max and His Money (page 50)

1. $15.00
2. 4 weeks
3. $55.00
4. $3.50

Who Sat Next to Whom? (page 51)

Accept any order as long as the same names are next to one another and the same names are sitting across from one another.

George Washington	Abraham Lincoln
Martin Luther King Jr.	John F. Kennedy

Number Cubes Addition Game (page 52)

Check that the number cubes have been added together correctly.

Week 5

Irregular Verbs (page 54)

1. bite: bit
2. eat: ate
3. break: broke
4. come: came
5. freeze: froze

The Milkmaid and Her Pail (page 55)

Check that response includes events in logical order.

Different Places (page 56)

Check that response includes a place that was different than expected. The response should also explain why.

Best Job in the World! (page 57)

Check that response includes drawings and symbols that represent the chosen job.

Multiplication Match-Up (page 58)

Multiplication equation Picture

Multiplication equation **Picture**

1. $5 \times 4 = 20$
2. $4 \times 5 = 20$
3. $2 \times 9 = 18$
4. $3 \times 7 = 21$

A
B
C
D

5. 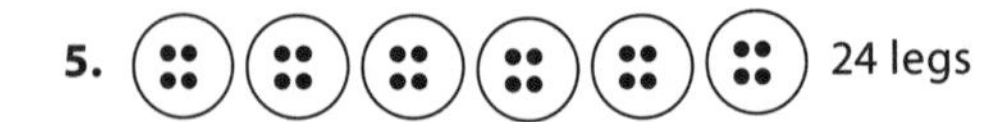 24 legs

Three-Dimensional Inventions (page 59)

Check that the answer includes a name for the invention, describes what the invention does, and includes a picture.

Measure Liters (page 60)

1. A
2. A
3. C
4. A
5. B

Who Says That? (page 61)

1. child
2. shoe salesperson/parent
3. bagger at a grocery store
4. waiter/waitress
5. doctor/parent/nurse
6. teacher

Answer Key *(cont.)*

The Best Parachute Design (page 62)

Check that each parachute has been made with the same materials and participate in the "test drop."

Week 6

Using the Dictionary (page 64)

Check the definitions of the selected words against a dictionary.

Save Our Park! (page 65)

1. B
2. C

What Do You Think? (page 66)

Check that response includes an opinion statement about the selected book, television show, or game, and that the response includes a closing sentence.

Puppy Prints Picture (page 67)

Check that drawing incorporates the puppy prints.

Measuring Practice (page 68)

1. 4 centimeters
   10 centimeters
   10 – 4 = 6 centimeters
2. 2 inches
   3 inches
   3 –2 = 1 inches

Fractions Fun (page 69)

Check that the fractions add up to 1.

Plotting Fractions (page 70)

1. True
2. True
3. False
4. False
5. 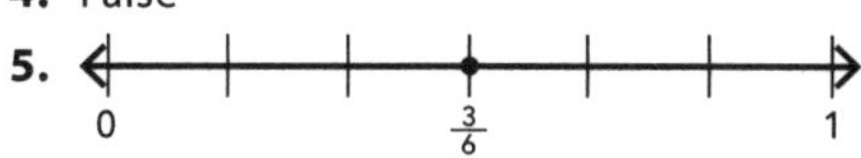

Explain: Answer should include that the number line has been partitioned into six equal parts, and the dot is placed where the third part is marked.

What Word Is It? (page 71)

1. nose
2. peach
3. ant
4. jar
5. bang

The Perfect 10 (page 72)

Check that the winner has reached 10 points.

Answer Key (cont.)

Week 7

Hunting for Suffixes! (page 74)

island(s)

slow(ly)

rest(ed)

breath(s)

cave(s)

bad(ly)

tri(ed)

sav(ed)

1. powerful: strong, effective
2. powerless: without power, helpless
3. repower: to power again
4. unpowered: not having or using power

Challenge: Check that answer includes ways to use word parts to define unknown words.

The Horned Owl (page 75)

1. in the woods and in town
2. rabbits, squirrels, and other birds
3. keeps the eggs warm and hunts for food

My Creature (page 76)

Check that poem is about an imagined creature.

Robot Orders (page 77)

Check that response includes drawings and words that explain what the robot would be ordered to do.

Picture Fractions (page 78)

1. $\frac{1}{4}$; one-fourth
2. $\frac{1}{4}$; one-fourth
3. $\frac{2}{3}$; two-thirds
4. $\frac{3}{4}$; three-fourths
5. $\frac{1}{3}$; one-third
6. $\frac{1}{2}$; one-half

Jog-A-Thon (page 79)

What Facts Do You Know?: Jen ran $\frac{2}{3}$ of a mile. Christina ran $\frac{3}{5}$ of a mile.

How Can You Solve?:

Jen:

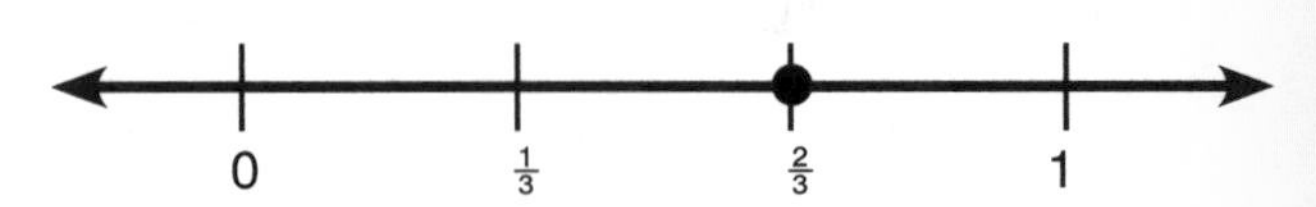

Christina:

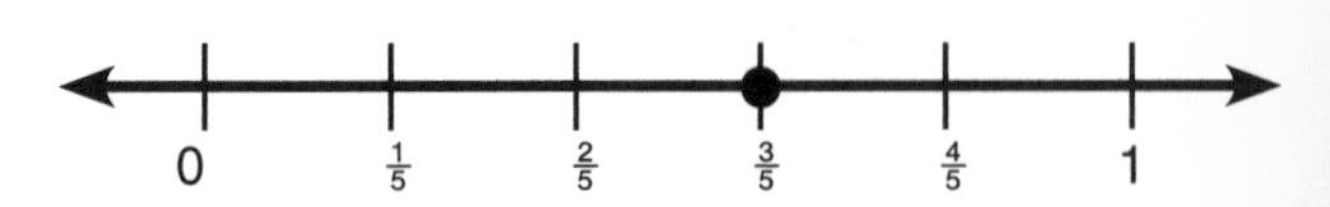

Did They Run the Same Distance?: No, they did not run the same distance.

Explain How You Know: Because $\frac{2}{3}$ and $\frac{3}{5}$ are not plotted on the same position on the number line, they are not equal.

Traffic Survey (page 80)

1. white
2. 1 more blue car
3. black

What Comes Next? (page 81)

1. afternoon
2. month
3. Friday
4. June
5. baby/infant

Turning Letters into Sentences (page 82)

Check that sentences include words that begin with the chosen letters.

Week 8

Noun or Verb? (page 84)

Nouns: ant, April, camera, eagle, holiday, joy, meal, ribbon, sky, spider, tree

Verbs: add, arrive, behave, decide, exclaim, forgive, imagine, prepare, prove

Answer Key *(cont.)*

The History of Death Valley (page 85)

5 Death Valley was made a national monument.

2 People came to Death Valley to mine gold.

4 Scotty's Castle was built.

1 American Indians came to Death Valley.

3 People came to Death Valley to mine borax.

Don't Throw It Away! (page 86)

Check that response three ways to reuse, repurpose, or recycle household items.

Slide Winner! (page 87)

Check that drawing incorporates the slide into a drawing of the home.

Perimeter (page 88)

1. 14
2. 24
3. 22
4. 18

Reading Bar Graphs (page 89)

Frequency Table (in order from left to right): 10; 8; 4; 1; 6; 2

1. 8
2. 4
3. 9
4. round candy
5. 8

Nick and Peyton (page 90)

What Facts Do You Know?: $\frac{4}{8}$ between 0 and 1 or between $\frac{3}{8}$ and $\frac{5}{8}$

How Can You Solve?:

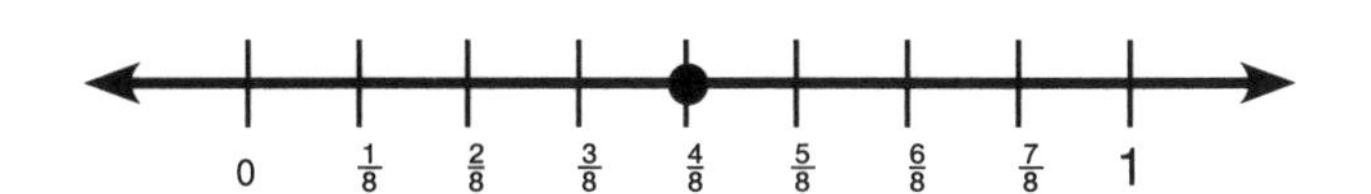

Who Is Correct?: Answer should include that Nick and Peyton are both right.

Explain How You Know: Answer should include that when the line is divided into eight equal parts, four of them are the same as half of them.

What Rhymes? (page 91)

1. go
2. story
3. park
4. cake
5. phone
6. table

Multiplication Card Game (page 92)

Check that multiplication has been calculated correctly.

Week 9

Contraction Action (page 94)

1. What's
2. it'll
3. they'd
4. there's
5. Who's
6. could've

Home Run (page 95)

Check that the pictures are in order as they occur in the story.

Answer Key *(cont.)*

Do We Need Chores? (page 96)

Check that response includes reasons to support why chores are or are not important.

The Most Unusual Restaurant (page 97)

Check that response includes what items will be on the menu, drawings or pictures to go with the items, and prices.

Estimating Measurements (page 98)

1. 11 centimeters
2. 4 inches

Digital and Analog (page 99)

Digital	Analog	Clock Face
11:15	quarter after 11; 15 minutes after 11	
6:50	10 minutes to 7	
12:45	quarter to 1; 15 minutes to 1	
5:55	5 minutes to 6	
3:11	11 minutes after 3	
4:49	11 minutes to 5	
6:34	26 minutes to 7	

Shape Riddles (page 100)

1. square
2. trapezoid
3. circle
4. pentagon
5. half circle

Verb Puzzlers (page 101)

shine	slip	sizzle
swimming	shower	scream

Guess the Number Game (page 102)

Check the correct guess with the "secret" number.

Parent Handbook

Dear Parents or Guardians,

Have you ever wondered why states have learning standards? Teachers used to determine what they would cover based on what content was included in their textbooks. That seems crazy! Why would educators put publishers in charge of determining what they should teach? Luckily, we've moved past that time period into one where educational professionals create standards. These standards direct teachers on what students should know and be able to do at each grade level. As a parent, it's your job to make sure you understand the standards! That way, you can help your child be ready for school.

The following pages are a quick guide to help you better understand both the standards and how they are being taught. There are also suggestions for ways you can help as you work with your child at home.

Here's to successful kids!

Sincerely,

The Shell Education Staff

College and Career Readiness Standards

Today's college and career readiness standards, including the Common Core State Standards and other national standards, have created more consistency among states in how they teach math and English language arts. In the past, state departments of education had their own standards for each grade level. The problem was, what was taught at a specific grade in one state may have been taught at a different grade in another state. This made it difficult when students moved from state to state.

Today, many states have adopted new standards. This means that for the first time, there is better consistency in what is being taught at each grade level across the states, with the ultimate goal of getting students ready to be successful in college and in their careers.

Standards Features

The overall goal for the standards is to better prepare students for life. Today's standards use several key features:

- They describe what students should know and be able to do at each grade level.
- They are rigorous.
- They require higher-level thinking.
- They are aimed at making sure students are prepared for college and/or their future careers.
- They require students to explain and justify answers.

Mathematical Standards

There are several ways that today's mathematics standards have shifted to improve upon previous standards. The following are some of the shifts that have been made.

Focus

Instead of covering a lot of topics lightly, today's standards focus on a few key areas at much deeper levels. Only focusing on a few concepts each year allows students more time to understand the grade-level concepts.

How Can You Help?	What Can You Say?
Provide paper or manipulatives (such as beans or pieces of cereal) as your child is working so that he or she can show his or her answer.	Is there another way you can show the answer?
Have your child explain his or her thinking or the way he or she got the answer.	What did you do to solve the problem? What were you thinking as you solved the problem?

Coherence

The standards covered for each grade are more closely connected to each other. In addition, each grade's standards are more closely connected to the previous grade and the following grade.

How Can You Help?	What Can You Say?
Help your child to make connections to other concepts he or she has learned.	What else have you learned that could help you understand this concept?
Ask your child to circle words that may help him or her make connections to previously learned concepts.	What words in the directions (or in the word problem) help you know how to solve the problem?

Fluency

The standards drive students to perform mathematical computations with speed and accuracy. This is done through memorization and repetition. Students need to know the most efficient way to solve problems, too!

How Can You Help?	What Can You Say?
Help your child identify patterns that will work for increasing speed and accuracy.	What numbers do you know that can help you solve this problem?
Encourage the most efficient way to solve problems.	Can you get the same answer in a different way? Is there an easier way to solve the problem?

Mathematical Standards *(cont.)*

Deep Understanding

Students must develop a very good understanding of mathematical concepts. A deep understanding of mathematical concepts ensures that students know the *how* and the *why* behind what they are doing.

How Can You Help?	What Can You Say?
Encourage your child to make a model of the answer.	How do you know your answer is correct? Can you show your answer in a different way?
Have your child explain the steps he or she uses to solve problems.	Can you teach me to solve the problem?

Application

Today's standards call for more rigor. Students need to have strong conceptual understandings, be able to use math fluently, and apply the right math skills in different situations.

How Can You Help?	What Can You Say?
Encourage your child to use multiple methods for solving and showing his or her answers.	Can you explain your answer in a different way?
Have your child circle words or numbers that provide information on how to solve the problem.	What words gave you clues about how to solve this problem?

Dual Intensity

Students need to develop good understandings of mathematical concepts and then practice those concepts.

How Can You Help?	What Can You Say?
Provide practice on concepts or basic facts your child is having trouble with.	What did you have difficulty with? How can you practice that?
Have your child identify where his or her breakdown in understanding is when solving a problem.	Where can you find the help you need?

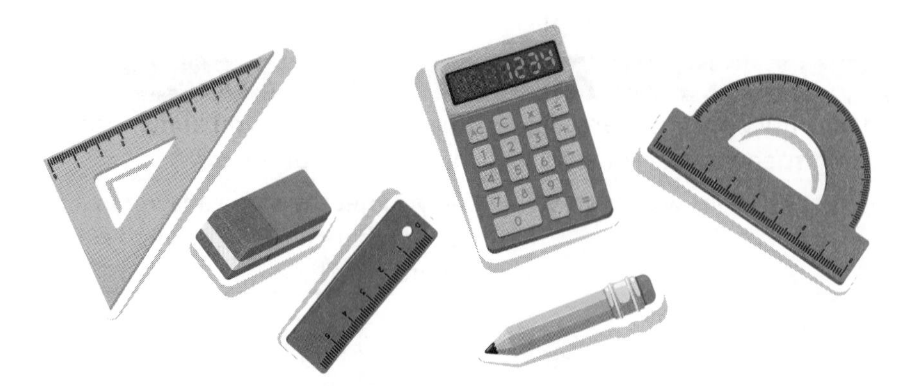

Language Arts Standards

The following charts describe the key shifts in language arts standards and some great ways that you can help your child achieve with them.

Balancing Informational and Literary Texts

Students should read and have books read aloud to them that represent a variety of texts and have a balance of informational and literary texts.

How Can You Help?	What Can You Say?
Find topics your child is interested in and then find both fiction and nonfiction books on the topic.	Since you like dinosaurs, let's find a story about dinosaurs and an informational book that tells facts about dinosaurs!
Encourage your child to know features of informational and literary texts.	How do you know this book is informational? What features does this literary book have?

Knowledge in the Disciplines

Once students reach sixth grade, they are expected to gain information directly through content-area texts rather than have the information told to them. Younger students can read nonfiction texts to prepare for this transition in the middle grades.

How Can You Help?	What Can You Say?
Talk about science and social studies topics with your child in everyday conversations so that your child learns about related words and concepts.	I heard on the news that there will be a lunar eclipse tonight. Let's watch it together so that we can see the shadow of Earth come between the moon and the sun.
Provide a variety of experiences for your child so that he or she can use them when reading about a topic. It makes the topic easier to understand.	Let's go have fun exploring the tide pools! What do you think we will see there? (*ask before*) What did you see at the tide pools? (*ask after*)

Staircase of Complexity

Students should read grade-appropriate complex texts. They may not understand the content right away, but with support and time, they will eventually comprehend what they're reading.

How Can You Help?	What Can You Say?
Know your child's reading level. Help your child find books that are at the high end of your child's reading level.	I found these three books for you to read. Which one interests you?
Read books to your child that are above his or her reading level. It exposes him or her to more complex vocabulary, sentences, and ideas.	Which book would you like me to read to you?

Language Arts Standards *(cont.)*

Text-Based Answers

Students should be able to answer questions and defend their positions using evidence from texts. This evidence can include illustrations and other graphics.

How Can You Help?	What Can You Say?
Ask your child to explain his or her answer using evidence from a book.	How do you know that? How else do you know ______?
Ask your child to look for evidence about something you notice in a book.	What evidence is there that ______?

Writing from Sources

Students should easily reference the texts they are reading as they write about them.

How Can You Help?	What Can You Say?
Have your child underline in the text the answers to questions her or she is answering through writing.	Where is the evidence in the text? How can you include that in your written response?
Provide sentence frames to help your child reference the text.	On page ______, the author says ______.

Academic Vocabulary

Academic vocabulary is a student's ability to recognize, understand, and use more sophisticated words in both reading and writing. Having a strong vocabulary allows students to access more complex texts.

How Can You Help?	What Can You Say?
Model using precise vocabulary.	I noticed you used the word ______. Could you have used a stronger word?
Provide a wide variety of experiences for your child to learn new words. These experiences don't have to cost money. They can be simple, everyday activities!	We are going to get the oil changed in the car. I want you to see if you can find the mechanic in his overalls.

Doodle

Doodle